THE ART OF
SPENDING MONEY

The
ART
of
SPENDING
MONEY

Simple Choices for a Richer Life

MORGAN HOUSEL

PORTFOLIO | PENGUIN

PORTFOLIO | PENGUIN
An imprint of Penguin Random House LLC
1745 Broadway, New York, NY 10019
penguinrandomhouse.com

Most Portfolio books are available at a discount when purchased in quantity for
sales promotions or corporate use. Special editions, which include personalized
covers, excerpts, and corporate imprints, can be created when purchased in
large quantities. For more information, please call (212) 572-2232 or e-mail
specialmarkets@penguinrandomhouse.com. Your local bookstore can also
assist with discounted bulk purchases using the Penguin Random House
corporate Business-to-Business program. For assistance in locating a
participating retailer, e-mail B2B@penguinrandomhouse.com.

BOOK DESIGN BY TANYA MAIBORODA

LIBRARY OF CONGRESS CATALOGING-IN-PUBLICATION DATA

Names: Housel, Morgan, author
Title: The art of spending money: simple choices for a richer life / Morgan Housel.
Description: New York, NY: Portfolio/Penguin, [2025] |
Includes bibliographical references.
Identifiers: LCCN 2025015949 (print) | LCCN 2025015950 (ebook) |
ISBN 9780593716625 (hardcover) | ISBN 9780593716632 (ebook)
Subjects: LCSH: Money—Psychological aspects | Wealth | Finance, Personal
Classification: LCC HG222.3 .H679 2025 (print) |
LCC HG222.3 (ebook) | DDC 332.024/01—dc23/eng/20250808
LC record available at https://lccn.loc.gov/2025015949
LC ebook record available at https://lccn.loc.gov/2025015950

ISBN 9798217048601 (international edition)

Printed in the United States of America

3rd Printing

The authorized representative in the EU for product safety and compliance
is Penguin Random House Ireland, Morrison Chambers, 32 Nassau Street,
Dublin D02 YH68, Ireland, https://eu-contact.penguin.ie.

For Kellie, the unicorn

Contents

Author's Note

When I wrote *The Psychology of Money*, I wanted to explore how we think about wealth and investing—how emotions and social pressures influence decisions that we pretend are purely rational.

This book, *The Art of Spending Money*, is a natural follow-up.

While *The Psychology of Money* focused on how we grow wealth, *The Art of Spending Money* focuses on how we use it.

Neither book tells you what to do with your money, because everyone's different. But both seek to understand what happens in our heads while using money. And here, we are far more alike.

The same big idea applies to both books: Money is less about numbers and more about stories—stories we tell ourselves about what matters, what makes us happy, and how we measure success.

Spending money is more art than science. There's no universal formula, no fixed rules. What brings one person joy may leave another feeling empty. And so, just as with investing, understanding our emotions—our biases, hopes, and fears—can guide us toward smarter choices. Choices that reflect who we are, what we value, and how we want to live.

If *The Psychology of Money* taught us how to earn freedom, this book is about learning how to make the most of it.

Here we go.

Introduction:
The Quest of the Simple Life

Dr. Dan Goodman once performed LASIK eye surgery on a woman looking to ditch her glasses. The patient returned for a checkup a few weeks later, despondent. She said the surgery ruined her life.

There was nothing wrong with the procedure—she could see clearly without glasses for the first time in years.

Goodman pressed: Then what's the problem?

The patient said she expected that after losing her glasses, her husband would find her more attractive and her coworkers would find her more intelligent. When she realized they didn't, and love and respect weren't driven by something superficial like her glasses, she was crushed.

"You have a problem I can't help you with," Goodman told her. "I'm sorry I didn't realize it earlier."

It's astounding to witness someone gain what they thought they always wanted only to realize that happiness is more complicated than they first assumed.

And, my gosh, that is so true with money.

There's an old saying that nothing's worse than getting what you want but not what you need. That sums up so many people's relationship with money and success. If you're lucky enough to get what you want (money), you might still realize it's not what you need (family, friends, health, being part of something bigger than yourself). And then you're disappointed. What could be worse?

This book is about how spending money has little to do with spreadsheets and numbers and a lot to do with psychology, envy, social aspirations, identity, insecurity, and other topics that are too often ignored in finance.

Can money buy happiness? Yes.

Can spending money make you happier? Yes.

But it's more complicated than many people think. In between the numbers, charts, and data sits the messiness and absurdity of the human mind. Money is a remarkable tool that can provide a better life if you know how to use it. But knowing how to use it is quite different from knowing how to acquire it.

Winston Churchill famously said that he got more out of alcohol than alcohol got out of him. By the same logic: I have seen rich people whose money got more out of them than they got from it, because they spent their life desperately chasing money without any sense of how to use it to make them happier. I have also seen low-income people get tremendous value out of what little money they had, using it as a source of leverage to acquire more of what made them happy.

What matters is not necessarily how much money you have. It's whether you understand and can control the psychology and behaviors that can make the connection between money and happiness more complicated than we assume.

There are so many ways that observation can affect your own life.

Think about the broke young person who buys a car he can't afford because he thinks it will bring respect and admiration from his peers.

Or someone who diligently saved their entire life but cannot bring themselves to spend a reasonable amount of money in retirement because "saver" has become ingrained as part of their identity.

Or the young couple saving for a down payment on a two-bedroom house whose expectations are suddenly inflated by a friend who just bought a three-bedroom house.

The rich entrepreneur who never feels like she has enough.

The low-wage worker who always feels like he has plenty.

None of these topics have to do with spreadsheets or numbers. They're so much messier than that. It's all psychology, sociology, and understanding how everyone's different. Understanding how everyone's just trying to make it through life the best they can, making sense of the world given the experiences they've had, who they want to be, and what they think others think of them.

In school, finance is taught as a science, with clean formulas and logical conclusions. But in the real world, money is an art.

I worked as a valet at a five-star hotel in Los Angeles during college. One day we hosted an invite-only high-end furniture show for the city's moneyed elite.

A man came out to the valet stand chatting with a friend about how he just spent $21,000 on an armchair. Several of my colleagues and I overheard him and were stunned. Spending that much on a chair—*a chair*—was inconceivable to us.

The guy saw our bewildered expressions and said: "Boys, I know. It's crazy. But when you have money, this is what you're supposed to do."

I found it such an interesting choice of words. "*Supposed to do.*" Did he actually like the chair? Or was he blindly pursuing what society told him he's supposed to like and how he should spend his money?

I remember then thinking, as a nineteen-year-old aspiring to be rich one day: Is that what *I'm* supposed to do one day? I'm supposed to study long hours in college and grind in a career for decades so I can tell my friends I bought an ugly chair that costs the equivalent of one half of an average household income?

Would that actually make me happier?

As I processed it all, I remember my reaction going from astonishment to amusement to almost feeling bad for the guy.

I got to know a lot of these people. It felt like so many of them had this mindless chase for wealth without actually knowing why they wanted it, other than the primal urge for more. They were very good at making money. But their ability to turn that money into a meaningfully better life felt rocky at best.

Of course, there's another path. Many people have figured out how to use money as a tool to provide things that actually make them happier in life. But the rich chair guy had it right: What society tells us we're supposed to do with money is not always what we should be doing to get the most out of it.

It's not our fault. A combination of evolution and social forces tell us—often in a shout—what we should want: more money than other people, bigger stuff than other people, shinier toys than other people. Sometimes that *is* what we want, and what you should chase. More often we will realize that spending money to show people how much money you have is a fast way to go broke and an expensive way to gain respect. Disappointment is often the outcome.

Now, I think you can use money to build a better life.

I think buying nice stuff can bring you joy.

I love ambition, hard work, and—most of all—independence.

But after writing about money for two decades, I am constantly amazed at how bad most of us are at knowing what we want out of money, or how to use it as anything more than a benchmark of status and success. And let me be clear: Most of this book is reflections I've had trying to figure out money and happiness in my own life.

If you ask parents what they wish for their kids, many will say, "I just want them to be happy."

Do you want them to be rich and successful? "Well, sure," they'll say, "but mostly I just want them to be happy."

That's great thinking. But many of those same parents, in their own lives, chase money and status at the expense of happiness. Perhaps the reason parents wish happiness over success for their children is because they've seen the downsides of blindly pursuing one over the other.

Carl Jung, one of the most influential psychologists to ever live, was once asked, "What do you consider to be more or less basic factors making for happiness in the human mind?" Jung listed them off:

1. Good physical and mental health.
2. Good personal and intimate relationships, such as those of marriage, the family, and friendships.
3. The faculty for perceiving beauty in art and nature.
4. Reasonable standards of living and satisfactory work.
5. A philosophic or religious point of view capable of coping successfully with the vicissitudes of life.

You can see how having money can affect some of those points. But money—especially lots of it—is not one of those points.

This book will not teach you how to spend money. If I (or anyone) could do that, it would be called *The Science of Spending Money*.

But I'm more interested in the *art* of spending money. Art can't be distilled into a one-size-fits-all formula. Art is complicated, often contradictory, and can be a window into your personality. The art of spending money covers things like individuality, greed, jealousy, status, and regret. That's what this book is about.

I try to tackle the art of spending money from several angles. But you'll find a few common denominators:

1. **There are two ways to use money.** One is as a tool to live a better life. The other is as a yardstick of status to measure yourself against others. Many people aspire for the former but spend their life chasing the latter.

2. **Money is a tool you can use. But if you're not careful, it will use you.** It will use you without mercy, and often without you even knowing it. For many people, money is both a financial asset and a psychological liability. Blind lust for more can hijack your identity, control your personality, and wedge out parts of your life that bring greater happiness.

3. **Spending money can buy happiness, but it's often an indirect path.** Money itself doesn't buy happiness, but it can help you find independence and purpose—both key ingredients for a happier life if you cultivate them. A big, nice house might make you happier, but mostly because it makes it easier to have friends and family over, and the friends and family are actually what are making you happy.

4. **Enduring happiness is found in contentment, so those happiest with money tend to be those who have found a way**

to stop thinking about it. You can value it, appreciate it, even marvel at it. But if money never leaves your mind, it's likely you've found yourself with an obsession, where it controls you. The best use of money is as a tool to leverage who you are, but never to define who you are.

5.   If you're confused about what a better life would look like, "one with more money" is an easy assumption. But that can sometimes mask deeper problems. Money is so tangible that it's an easy goal to strive for, and pursuing it can become the path of least resistance for those who haven't discovered what truly feeds their soul.

6.   Everyone can spend money in a way that will make them happier. But there is no universal formula on how to do it. The nice stuff that makes me happy might seem crazy to you, and vice versa. Debates over what kind of lifestyle you should live are often just people with different personalities talking over each other. Author Luke Burgis puts it another way: "After meeting our basic needs as creatures, we enter into the human universe of desire. And knowing what to want is much harder than knowing what to need."

In his 1907 book *The Quest of the Simple Life,* William Dawson writes about how many of his London peers devoted their lives to money and success but still seemed miserable. Those who lived simple lives in the country were comparatively jubilant.

His main observation was that those who were trying to get more money were actually held captive by it. They were so obsessed with wealth that it held control over their sanity, their relationships, their quality of life. What they intended to be a strategy to live a better life often became an ideology they were beholden to, like an invisible dictator. They wanted to have more money so they could become happier. But money could buy them everything except the ability to not be obsessed with money, which led to constant anxiety, which led to unhappiness. It was a vicious cycle. And most of them were blind to it.

Sometimes the stuff you spend money on has so much influence over your behavior that it's not clear whether you own things or the things own you. Benjamin Franklin put this so well when he wrote: "Many a man thinks he is buying pleasure, when he is really selling himself a slave to it."

Dawson wrote that the ideal life was a simple life. A simple life might still be extravagant, with fancy homes and luxuries and toys galore. But it's simple in the sense that money serves you, not the other way around. The kind of lifestyle you choose to live almost doesn't matter—what matters is that you actually choose it, rather than being addicted to the mere appeal of it. Dawson wrote that his goal was not to make a living; it was to make a life, and only a fool would sacrifice his actual life for the endless pursuit of an imaginarily better one.

The quest of your own simple life—however you choose to live it—starts with a deep understanding and examination of yourself. We'll begin there, in the next chapter, with a story about making sense of misfit children.

THE ART OF
SPENDING MONEY

ALL BEHAVIOR MAKES SENSE
WITH ENOUGH INFORMATION

Most debates about what's worth spending money on are actually just people with different life experiences talking over each other.

An important question I love is: What have you experienced that I haven't that makes you believe what you do? And would I believe the same if I experienced what you have?

It applies to so many things in life. Including money.

The most important topic in spending money, one that's the cause of so much financial frustration and disappointment, is that there is no "right" way to do it. There are no universal laws of what kind of spending will make everyone happy and fulfilled.

What I like spending money on might make no sense to you. My fears might be your joys. Your goal might be the thing I most want to avoid.

There's a saying: Never make fun of someone for mispronouncing a word, because it means they learned it from reading. As a corollary: Never make fun of how someone spends their money, because they learned it from living.

Everyone is a product of their own unique past. To understand why people spend the way they do, you have to dig deep into their life experiences.

My brother-in-law is a social worker. He works with kids from the lowest levels of abject poverty and broken homes who are pushed in and out of the foster system.

A lot of these kids struggle at school. Their behavior is poor. They skip class. They don't pay attention. They get into fights on the playground. They can't focus on the future.

It is easy for people to not only criticize these kids' behavior but shake their head in confusion.

"Why are you acting this way?" "Why can't you understand that if you behave better, you'll have a better future?" "How could you possibly think that's an OK thing to do?"

But there's a saying inside the foster care system: All behavior makes sense with enough information.

Once you understand what some of these kids have dealt with at home—the uncertainty, the lack of security, love, and attention—their behavior begins to make sense. They're in constant survival mode and never learned some of the basic social skills other kids take for granted.

You don't want to encourage or even justify their behavior. But once you see the world through their eyes, you quickly understand why someone would make decisions that seem foreign to you and me.

All behavior makes sense with enough information—including behavior about the different ways we spend our money.

By the late 1920s, America was at the tail end of a full social and economic cycle. The devastation of World War I was followed by a crippling recession. And then, after a decade of misery—finally—people got to relish an economic boom that gave name to the Roaring '20s.

Roaring doesn't do it justice—it was an absolute party. For a good five years in the mid 1920s the economy was fueled by cheap debt, a stock market bubble, and bootlegged liquor.

In June of 1928, syndicated columnist Robert Quillen wrote a newspaper headline that in fourteen words describes something so simple and important:

> The More You Were Snubbed While Poor, the More You Enjoy Displaying Your Wealth.
> By ROBERT QUILLEN

That's it. So much of the late-1920s desire to show off wealth with new cars, new clothes, new toys, was driven by a reaction to the poverty and uncertainty that preceded it.

When you at one time feel held back, then suddenly feel released, a common reaction is to frantically sprint ahead to make up for lost time. Historian Frederick Lewis Allen wrote about the era:

> Like the suddenly liberated vacationist, the country felt that it ought to be enjoying itself

more than it was, and that life was futile and nothing mattered much. But in the meantime it might as well play—follow the crowd, take up the new toys that were amusing the crowd.

People seemed to justify wild, unsustainable spending because they were making up for being snubbed and suppressed during the dour years. It felt as if they were righting a wrong, like getting revenge. They weren't spending wildly because they crunched the numbers and determined it was the right thing to do. They were trying to heal an emotional wound.

That behavior is timeless, and explains so much.

A close family member grew up extremely poor and in a broken home, snubbed in every way. He then became a successful businessman. When his daughter was preparing to go to college, he told her, "Pick the most expensive school you get into." Sending his daughter to an expensive school was such a powerful symbol of what he had overcome that, in his mind, it was almost as if he preferred to pay the most absurd price he could. High tuition was like a social trophy that made him feel great about the arc of his life.

If you didn't grow up snubbed, or snubbed in a different way, that might make no sense to you. But that's the point: A lot of spending makes no sense until you peel back the onion layers of someone's personality, identifying the specific thing they're trying to accomplish, or the hole they're trying to fill.

How your past influences your spending decisions can

manifest in different ways, with opposite outcomes depending on the person. Tiffany Aliche—a former preschool teacher who became a wildly successful financial educator—once said that she suffers from "post-traumatic broke syndrome." It's made it hard for her to spend her newfound wealth. "I was broke for so long, and it was so hard, that I'm afraid of going back there," she says.

If you try to make sense of spending habits—yours or other people's—you have to start with the understanding that people don't just spend money on things they find fun or useful. Their decisions often reflect the social and psychological experiences of their life. And since life experiences vary dramatically from person to person, what makes sense to you might seem crazy to me, and vice versa.

Spending a ton of money on a college degree might feel like a waste to one person, a nonnegotiable requirement to another, and the ultimate sign of climbing the social ladder to another. The same product has very different meanings to different people.

To someone who grew up in an old-money affluent family, a Lamborghini might be a symbol of gaudy egotism; to those who grew up with nothing, the car might serve as the ultimate symbol that you've made it.

No one should pretend that there's one right answer to these questions, because they fill a different psychological need for different people.

A lawyer who works one hundred hours a week and hates their job may have an urge to spend frivolously in an attempt to compensate for the misery of how their paycheck was earned. Never have I seen money burn a hole in someone's pocket faster than an investment banker receiving their annual bonus. After twelve months of Excel modeling until 3 a.m., you have an urge to prove to yourself that it was worth it, offsetting what you sacrificed. It's like someone held underwater for a minute—they do not take a calm breath when they surface; they gasp. A lot of spending is gasping. Related: I have noticed that those most capable of delayed gratification are often those who enjoy their work. The pay might be good, but the urge to compensate for your hard work with heavy spending isn't there.

The important point in all of this: Most debates about what's worth spending money on are actually just people with different life experiences talking over each other. How much you should spend, and why other people spend the way they do, starts to make sense when you accept that people who have lived different lives than you have want different things than you might.

I think it's a sign of deep immaturity to think that because you like spending your money a certain way, other people should too. It's a sign of deep immaturity to think that because you don't value something, no one else should either. That's not how the world works. What's reasonable and fulfilling spending to you might seem pointless to me. What's mandatory to me might seem like a waste to you.

The software engineer Billy Markus says, "People are not rational. They are rationalizing. Once you understand this simple fact, all the oddest human behavior will suddenly make way more sense."

It's why spending money should be viewed as an art, not a science. There are no universal answers on how to do it, or what's worth it. The best we can do is come up with a broad understanding of how varied people's minds can be, and how varied our preferences are for spending money.

———

Psychologist Lisa Feldman Barrett studies where emotions come from.

The classic view in psychology is that emotions are deeply ingrained at birth, the result of eons of evolution dictating that what's scary or funny or insulting to me should be the same for you—and all humans.

Barrett has spent three decades showing reality is more complex.

"Emotions are not built into your brain at birth," she says. "They are built by your brain as you need them."

From the moment you're born you begin to learn that this thing is scary, that thing is funny, or this thing should make you angry. You're even taught how to respond—contort your face this way when you're angry to get your point across to another person.

The important thing is that emotions are *learned*. They are a product of the culture and environment we are raised in. Barrett writes:

> Concepts like "Anger" and "Disgust" are not ge-
> netically predetermined. Your familiar emotion

concepts are built-in only because you grew up in a particular social context where those emotion concepts are meaningful and useful, and your brain applies them outside your awareness to construct your experiences.

The wild thing is to contemplate how different people's life experiences can be.

An impoverished child in Africa grows up learning to be scared of different things than a rich child in California. A kid from Manhattan grows up learning to seek joy from different things than a farmer in Iowa. The most basic and seemingly fundamental feelings of joy, fear, shame, and pride vary from culture to culture, family to family, person to person.

Behavior that embarrasses you might make me proud.

What I fear might be a thrill to you.

Your goals might be my nightmares.

And it's not just emotions that vary. What's *common sense* to one culture can seem absurd and backward to another. Psychologist Jonathan Haidt points out that a twenty-five-year-old son addressing his father by his first name is perfectly acceptable in America but deemed morally wrong—universally wrong—by other cultures. You find similar gaps when asking basic questions about food preparation, hygiene, how to raise kids, and how to treat your spouse. If you define "common sense" as truths that everyone agrees on, you'll find it to be rather uncommon, constrained to scientifically objective things like 2 + 2 = 4. Author David

McRaney notes that "consensus realities are mostly the result of geography."

All of this leads to extreme differences in people's views over what is worthwhile risk, a fun little experiment, a harmless guilty pleasure, or a fulfilling need.

Take an extreme example from the author Rob Henderson, who cycled through ten different foster homes growing up and went on to receive a PhD in psychology from Cambridge:

> A well-heeled student at an elite university can experiment with cocaine and will probably be just fine. A kid from a dysfunctional home with absentee parents is more likely to ride that first hit of meth to self-destruction. This may explain why a 2019 survey conducted by the Cato Institute found that more than 60 percent of Americans with at least a bachelor's degree were in favor of legalizing drugs, while less than half of Americans without a college degree thought it was a good idea. Drugs may be a recreational pastime for the rich, but for the poor they are often a gateway to further pain.

Back to my brother-in-law, the social worker.

He once told me a story about trying to convince a poor husband and wife about the value in saving even a small amount of money to avoid being evicted from their apartment the following month.

"They laughed at me," he said.

"Oh, you're a *future thinker*," the husband said, laughing harder.

"A what?" my brother-in-law said.

"A future thinker. You have the luxury of thinking about the future. We don't. Our vision of the future is the next twenty-four hours. Sometimes it's a five-minute window, like where we are going to get the next meal. That's as far ahead as we think."

They were spending every cent they could as fast as they could in part because the *entire concept* of "the future" was different from what yours or mine might be. There was no common ground on what might be considered common sense.

Tom Gayner, CEO of Markel Group, once told a story about having lunch with his daughter, a public-defense lawyer. Asked about a recent case, Gayner's daughter described a man who walked into a restaurant, ordered a meal, ate it, then tried to pay with literal Monopoly money.

"Was the guy stupid or a jerk or trying to play a joke?" Gayner asked.

"Daddy, he was poor and he was hungry," she said. "My clients are Zen masters of the right-now. There is no past. There is no future. He was hungry."

It's a radical example, but all of us—you, me, everyone—lives some version of it. There are so many instances—among rich and poor people alike—highlighting the idea that your values are equal to your preferences, and your preferences come from trying to reconcile your current needs with the lessons learned from your unique past experiences.

———————

Which brings me to two pieces of advice, both critical to understanding the art of spending money:

1. Don't let anyone tell you what you should or shouldn't spend money on. There is no "right" way. You have to figure out what makes you happy and fulfilled (more on that later).

"Personal finance is more *personal* than it is *finance*," says financial advisor Tim Maurer. It's one of the smartest money quotes I've ever heard.

A lot of money problems come from people spending or saving money in a way they think they're supposed to but that doesn't match their personality. They look for a one-size-fits-all answer to a problem that's deeply personal. It's like going through life forcing yourself to be someone you're not.

Most people understand if you like Italian food but my favorite is Mexican food, neither of us is right or wrong; it's just preference.

But that logic can go out the window when you extend it to what kind of house you live in, what clothes you wear, when you should retire, how often you travel or eat at restaurants. No matter how you live, plenty of people—friends, family, coworkers, online trolls—are quick and eager to tell you you're doing it wrong.

It's not until you acknowledge how personal and emotional our relationship with money can be that you realize you're on this journey alone. Maybe your spouse and your kids are part of the equation, but at some point you have to find your own way, fearless of what others think of it.

2. Be careful judging how other people spend their money.

Comedian George Carlin once said, "Everyone driving slower than you is an idiot, and everyone driving faster than you is a maniac!" It's natural to view everyone's decisions as wrong when they differ from yours.

There are times in this book when I criticize other people's spending decisions. But I try to restrain those criticisms to times when I think it's obvious that someone is spending money in a way that's detrimental to their own happiness.

It's one thing if someone doesn't understand the consequences of the decisions they make. They might need help and guidance. It's quite another to criticize someone's decisions only because they're different from yours.

It can be hard for some people to understand why you can't see things the way they do. I get why this happens: If I make a decision to live a different lifestyle than you do, you might view it as an attack on the decision you've made— especially if you have lingering doubts or uncertainty about your decision, which we all do.

The danger is that if I criticize how you spend money, I

might convince myself that there *is* one right way to spend—the way I do it. But that might prevent me from being more introspective about my own decisions, or wondering if I could do better, or trying to understand my own emotions. Judging others requires bullheaded confidence, which can prevent you from growing.

A healthy financial philosophy is having respect for others' experiences, an appreciation of your own, and an understanding that all behavior makes sense with enough information.

Now, let me tell you another story about respect and admiration.

MAY I HAVE YOUR ATTENTION PLEASE

You think you want nice stuff, but what you really want is respect, admiration, and attention.

I f you're confused about what a better life would look like, "one with more money" is an easy assumption.

It's such a simple idea that influences so many people. "Living a good life" is one of the most complicated topics that philosophers have debated for thousands of years. And "more money" is such an easy and quantifiable thing to chase.

But the desire for more money and the things it can buy often obscures what you actually want: respect and admiration from other people.

An easy connection to make is that if you had more money, you could buy a nicer car and a bigger house, and if you had a nicer car and a bigger house, people would respect and admire you more.

Sometimes they will. But let me share my personal take.

I've written letters to both of my kids hoping to pass along a few financial lessons I've learned in life. Something I wrote to both of them is that you might think you want a nicer car and a bigger house, but I'm telling you, you don't.

What you actually want is respect and admiration from other people, and you think that having nice stuff will bring it.

But it rarely does—at least as much as you expected—especially from the people you want respect and admiration from.

I love the idea of something called the reverse obituary.

Try this: Write down what you want your obituary to say, then figure out how to live up to it.

It's the cleanest, simplest way to plot out what you want in life and what truly matters.

Everyone's self-written obituary will be different. But I suspect most people would want theirs to say: You were loved. You were respected. You were admired. You were helpful. You were a good parent, a good spouse, a caring friend. You were an asset to your community. You made a contribution to your industry. You were wise, funny, and smart.

Now realize what's not in there.

Almost no one in this exercise would think about their obituary mentioning how much horsepower their car has, how many square feet their home is, or how much they spent on clothes. Your salary would not be mentioned, nor how many carats are in your wedding ring, nor that you re-did your kitchen with imported Italian marble.

I like nice things. I have some fancy things. But I'm always struck by the contrast here of what people want versus what they aspire to.

The reason few material things would make their way into your ideal obituary is because you inherently know those things don't actually matter.

In his book *Status Anxiety*, Alain de Botton writes that "the predominant impulse behind our desire to rise in the social hierarchy may be rooted not so much in the material goods we can accrue or the power we can wield as in the amount of love we stand to receive as a consequence of high status."

We view nice stuff as the ticket to what we actually desire: attention.

This is not a modern realization. It has little to do with social media or people becoming more materialistic. It's a deeply human reaction. The great economist Adam Smith wrote in 1759: "To what purpose is all the toil and bustle of this world? What is the end of avarice and ambition, of the pursuit of wealth, of power and pre-eminence? Is it to supply the necessities of nature?"

Of course not, Smith reasoned, because even low-wage workers in his time had food, shelter, and families.

What drives them, Smith wrote, was that "to be observed, to be attended to, to be taken notice of with sympathy, complacency, and approbation, are all the advantages which we can propose to derive from it. It is the vanity, not the ease, or the pleasure, which interests us."

It's an astonishing statement: We value the attention

money brings us more than we value the comfort and convenience of stuff that money can buy.

This idea applies to different people with different intensities. And even if you accept that the desire for nice stuff is a strategy to gain attention, I think it's fair to say: So what? If respect and attention are what I desire, and having an awesome car provides it, what's the problem?

Maybe there's no problem, but let me make a more nuanced point: There are cases when people's desire to show off fancy stuff is because it's their *last remaining* or even *only* way to gain respect and admiration. If you struggle to gain respect and admiration through your intelligence, humor, empathy, or capacity for love, you might default to the only remaining—and least effective—lever: your stuff. Look at my car, *beep beep, vroom vroom.*

The three most important variables when seeking different ways to get people's attention—a prerequisite for them to respect and admire you—are: How effective is it, how durable is it, and who's paying attention?

To break down each:

How effective is it? Spending money on nice things might be the quickest way to get someone's attention, because it's visible, public, and doesn't require talking to anyone.

How durable is it? If I'm impressed with your car today, I might give you a little attention. But tomorrow the shock wears off a little. A month from now I yawn when I see your car. A year from now I couldn't care less.

Who's paying attention? Mostly strangers, and even then there's a subtle point that when a stranger notices your car, they're gawking at the car, not at you. Does your spouse notice your car? Your parents? Your close friends? Your kids? Of course, but it's probably the last thing they use to measure how much they respect and admire you. They tend to care much more about how kind, funny, intelligent, helpful, and loving you are.

So spending money is probably the fastest way to get attention, but it's not durable attention, and it's probably the least effective toward the people whose respect and admiration you actually desire. It's like junk food: very tempting, immediately satisfying, but long-term damaging.

The point is not to say don't bother trying to gain attention with your car, home, or clothes. Social signaling is important to fitting in and doing well in life. But once you view spending money on stuff to gain people's attention as the junk food of respect and admiration, the desire to keep spending on things that just show off how successful you are diminishes.

My guess is that if your favorite comedian, actor, or athlete turned out to be broke, your opinion of them wouldn't change that much. It wouldn't impact how much you admire them, because you admire them for talents money can't buy.

Former football player Chad Johnson once explained why some people think he's cheap: There's no need to show off your material wealth when your name is so big that people already respect and admire you for your talents alone:

> If you can get to a point in your career where your name becomes bigger than anything you can purchase, there's your value.
>
> There is nothing I can buy that is bigger than my name alone. So it made no sense [to buy jewelry]. *I'm me.* It's pointless.

Even when Amazon was huge and successful, Jeff Bezos used to drive a Honda Accord. Today he has a $500 million yacht. Is he respected and admired more for it? Not in the slightest. He could ride a cheap bicycle and people would admire him for being the greatest entrepreneur of our era, because that's what he is. Steve Jobs lived in a home that didn't have any furniture. It didn't matter. He was an icon.

These are all famous people, extreme examples. But for us ordinary folks, there's so much to learn from this. If you gain your respect and admiration for who you are rather than what you own, your desire to spend more money on flashy things plunges.

The same is probably true for the people you admire most. I love and admire my parents, and let me tell you it's not because of their clothes. Isn't there so much to learn from that? Shouldn't gaining respect and admiration through what you do instead of what you own be the goal?

In her book, *Never Enough*, author Jennifer Breheny Wallace writes that "pride can be felt two ways: intrinsically, when you're authentically proud of yourself; and extrinsically, when another's opinions tell you how you should feel, what psychologists call hubristic pride."

So much modern spending is an attempt to foster the latter. But so much of the deep, fulfilling pride we naturally crave comes from the former: being proud of who you are and what you've done more than what you're wearing or driving. Perhaps most importantly, psychologist Tim Kasser once pointed out that those who most value extrinsic pride have less bandwidth to pursue intrinsic pride.

It's like those chasing junk food (material status) have less remaining appetite for nourishing food (family, friends, intelligence, humor, love). In long-term studies, those who valued extrinsic pride the most were more likely to end up anxious, depressed, and to abuse alcohol.

The desire to show off can be so natural. I've noticed that the people who most aspire to own fancy sports cars tend to be young people, especially young men. Perhaps when you're young without much life experience, your ability to gain respect through your wisdom, intelligence, and love is lower than it will be later in life, so you naturally gravitate to your last remaining option: material possessions.

I have felt this so clearly in my own life. My dream to one day own a Ferrari was high when I was young, dumb, had zero social skills and even fewer job skills. Today I am completely content with my more modest car, and aspire to gain respect and admiration by being a good father, husband,

and decent writer—things I had no chance of offering the world when I was twenty years old.

The danger comes when you underestimate what people actually value you for. I have a good friend I've known for decades. He's one of my favorite people. He also happens to earn a decent, but not substantial, living. It bothers him, and he often talks about how it makes him feel lesser than some of his peers. One day I told him: If you're a good dad, a good husband, an honest person, a hard worker, a helpful friend, and a funny joke-teller, you've probably earned 98 percent of the respect and admiration that I am capable of giving you. If you also happened to be rich and successful, I might bump that up to 99 percent or something. But let's not pretend that it makes much difference. I like you for who you are, not how much money you earn or the car you drive.

Once you see people being respected and admired for reasons that have nothing to do with material possessions, you begin to wonder why you have such a strong desire for those possessions. Everyone's different—all behavior makes sense with enough information—but I tend to view my own material desire as a loose proxy for the inverse of what else I have to offer the world. The higher my desire for fancy stuff, the less real value I have to offer for things that actually make me happy.

It's a simple idea that keeps my priorities in view.

Whose respect and admiration do I want? Mostly my family's and close friends'.

What do they pay the most attention to? How I make them feel, how I treat them, and how helpful I can be.

Do they care about my nice stuff? Meh, not so much.

It's so easy.

Two things I try to keep in mind here:

1. **Observe what actually makes you happy and maximize that.**

Like many people, I've seen a range of income during my career. What strikes me is that the things that make me happy with a higher income are the same things that made me happy with a much lower income: spending time with my family, doing things outdoors, a long chat with a friend. If flying first-class to a five-star resort and building sandcastles on the beach with my kids is a 10, playing LEGOs with my kids on the living room floor of a small apartment was still a solid 8 or 9.

I love nice vacations, look forward to them, and spend more on them now that I have a higher income than I did a decade ago. But once you identify what about those vacations makes you happy, the thing you're pursuing might subtly shift in ways that put you closer to your ultimate goal—in this case, from "I should spend more money on vacations" to "I should spend more quality time with my family."

2. **Show off the inside of your house, not the outside.**

You don't have to take that idea—which I borrowed from author Robert Greene—literally. But the concept is helpful, that if you want to be proud of your success and display it with nice stuff, make it most visible to those whose respect and admiration you desire the most. I love the idea that my friends and family can benefit from the nice things I've purchased. I care far less about what strangers might think if they happen to see those things.

Another important point here: You might think that displaying your success to strangers is bringing you attention and admiration. But often the emotion it's actually stirring up in others is envy.

Ben Franklin used to say that one of the tricks in life is realizing that people will admire you more if they aren't jealous of you. It can be hard to tell when the transition between admiration and jealousy takes place, and it's common for a flashy person to think they are being admired when they are actually envied.

This is especially true when what made you rich was some form of advertising your success in a way that made others want to help and support you. When admiration turns to envy, that support dwindles, and people's tolerance for your errors shrinks.

Keep that in mind if you race up the social ladder, seeking attention along the way. Are you, in the process, making others envious of you? And is that a liability you are overlooking in your blind quest for more?

Dutch political philosopher Jan-Willem van der Rijt has a good saying here: "The appetite for applause counts amongst the lowest of human character traits."

Columnist David Brooks once made the distinction between "resume virtues" and "eulogy virtues."

Resume virtues are things like salary, job title, net worth, and how fancy your possessions are.

Eulogy virtues can be boiled down to how much people actually respect and admire you.

I've always thought it to be a profound point when choosing what to pursue in life, and thinking about that reverse obituary.

Warren Buffett—one of the richest men in history, who could literally buy anything he wanted—once said, "When you get to my age, you'll really measure your success in life by how many of the people you want to have love you actually do love you."

He went on: "That's the ultimate test of how you have lived your life. The trouble with love is that you can't buy it. You can buy sex. You can buy testimonial dinners. You can buy pamphlets that say how wonderful you are. But the only way to get love is to be lovable. It's very irritating if you have a lot of money. You'd like to think you could write a check: I'll buy a million dollars' worth of love. But it doesn't work that way."

MAYBE YOU ALREADY
HAVE ENOUGH

One of the most powerful money tales is the parable of the Mexican fisherman.

An American businessman visits Mexico and meets a local fisherman. The American is shocked to learn the fisherman only works a few hours a day.

"What do you do with the rest of your time?" the American asks.

"I sleep late, hang out with my family, read, take naps, and play guitar with my friends," the fisherman says.

"You're doing this all wrong. I have an idea," says the American. "You should work all day. Borrow money and buy another boat. Hire more fishermen to work for you. You could make so much money you'll be retired in ten years."

"What would I do in retirement?" the fisherman asks.

"You could sleep late, hang out with your family, read, take naps, and play guitar with your friends," says the American.

THE HAPPIEST PEOPLE
I KNOW

If your expectations grow faster than your income,
you will never be happy with your money.

When you dream about being happier in the future, you're probably imagining yourself being content with what you have. Maybe you imagine yourself enjoying a new house and an expensive lifestyle—but what you're actually doing is imagining yourself being content with those things, expecting nothing more and enjoying what's in front of you.

That's what feels good. That's the feeling you're chasing.

When actual experiences create less joy than you anticipated, it's often because the moment you acquire something new you immediately jump to desiring whatever else you don't have.

True happiness is when you stop asking what else you need to be happy. When you think of it like that, you become eager to spend less time asking what's missing and more time enjoying what you already have—regardless of how much or how little that might be. You realize that the key to happiness is being content with what you have, and its antidote is focusing on what you don't.

Marcel Proust once told the story of a young man who spent his day in envy, dreaming about the lives of the rich and famous aristocrats. The young man would go to museums and gawk at pictures of mansions, luxury, and splendor, agonizing over the life he didn't have.

Proust then told the young man to spend his time focusing on the artist Jean Siméon Chardin. Chardin painted scenes of everyday life—food, animals, nature. The point was to learn to appreciate objects that the man already had in front of him. To learn to appreciate the life he had rather than to dwell on the dream life he didn't.

"When you walk around a kitchen, you will say to yourself, this is interesting, this is grand, this is beautiful like a Chardin," Proust wrote.

Appreciating what's in front of you rather than dwelling on what you don't have. What a wonderful analogy for money too.

The happiest people I know are the most content.

Not necessarily the richest, the healthiest, the most beautiful, or the most successful. Just whoever gets to a point of saying, "I'm good, I'm satisfied with what I have and who I am." That's nirvana. That's who takes the happiness crown.

Many of these people do have a lot of money. Some of them spend a lot of money and live incredible material lives.

But I often think about my grandmother-in-law, who spent three decades in retirement with very little money, living off a meager Social Security check and nothing else. She was technically on the verge of poverty. But in her head, she had everything she needed and wanted—she was perfectly content in her small garden and reading books from the library. She had little, but wanted even less.

And she was one of the happiest people you could have ever met.

I've met half a dozen billionaires in my life—not a single one was as happy as my grandmother-in-law. It was so easy to see why: Her low expectations gave her a sense of contentment, which in turn became an enormous source of psychological wealth that some of the richest people in the world lack.

Psychological wealth is such an important concept, and with money it comes from proper expectations. Happiness is contentment. Contentment is what you have relative to what you want.

Everyone's life follows that formula, in one direction or another.

All happiness in life is just the gap between expectations and circumstances. The person who has everything but wants even more feels poorer than the person who has little but wants nothing else. How could it be any different?

That's not a plea to live like a monk. You can have a huge house, an expensive car, take incredible vacations—and be content with all of it, appreciating it and desiring nothing more. That can be an amazing life.

The key is realizing that happiness is the state when nothing is missing, regardless of the lifestyle you're living.

The more you say to yourself, "I would be happier if I had this new car," the more you're just focusing on the fact that you're not happy right now. Desire is a hidden form of debt that must be repaid before you get to feel any happiness.

Irish novelist Iris Murdoch brilliantly framed the curse of not appreciating what you have: "People from a planet without flowers would think we must be mad with joy the whole time to have such things about us."

But are we? Of course not. When you don't appreciate what you already have and only focus on what's missing, nothing ever feels good enough. Happiness remains elusive.

There's a Stoic saying: "Not needing wealth is more valuable than wealth itself." So much of the art of spending money, and being happier with your money, is taking that wisdom to heart.

———

Nothing is as desired as much as the thing you want but can't have.

In fact, for most people there's a hierarchy of spending that goes something like this:

- If you don't want something and don't have it, you don't think about it.
- If you want something and have it, you might feel OK.
- If you want something and don't have it, you might feel motivated.

- If you want something and can't have it, you drive yourself absolutely mad.

Consider this idea from the financial advisor Peter Mallouk:

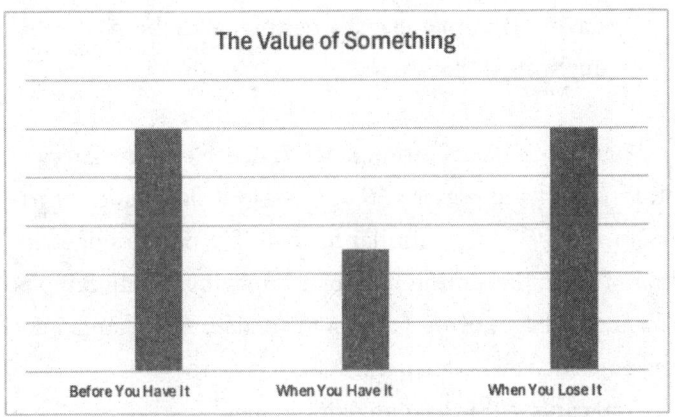

It hardly matters what the "something" here is—a glass of water to a thirsty person is more valuable than a private jet is to a billionaire who has two others.

This all makes sense when you understand what your brain wants.

By and large, your brain doesn't want nice cars or big homes.

It wants dopamine.

That's it.

Your brain just wants dopamine.

I'll leave it to the excellent book *The Molecule of More* to describe the process:

Dopamine is the chemical of desire that always asks for more—more stuff, more stimulation, and more surprises.

In pursuit of these things, it is undeterred by emotion, fear, or morality.

From dopamine's point of view, it's not the having that matters; it's getting something—anything—that's new.

Your brain doesn't want stuff. It doesn't even want new stuff. It wants to *engage in the process and anticipation of getting new stuff*. This is similar to actor Will Smith's description of fame: Becoming famous is amazing. Being famous is a mixed bag. Losing fame is miserable. The change, not the amount, is what matters.

You can see this so often with money.

When you're young, you dream about having a car—*any car.*

When you get a $10,000 car, you dream of the $20,000 car.

When you get a $20,000 car, you dream of the $50,000 car.

If you get the $50,000 car, you dream of the $100,000 car.

If you get the $100,000 car, you dream of having several $100,000 cars.

There's almost no end to this. The millionaires look at the centimillionaires, who look at the billionaires, who look at the decabillionaires, who look at the centibillionaires. And what do the centibillionaires want? Immortality.

It's always just *What's next? What's missing? How can I*

get to the next level? That's what you do because that's what your brain wants.

After winning gold medals or championships, a lot of athletes will tell you the emotion they felt wasn't elation. It was *relief.* Their own expectations, and the expectations of others, were so high that winning the ultimate prize merely got them to psychological par. Then their focus immediately shifts to what they don't have: winning the next competition.

A few years after leaving office, former President Richard Nixon mentioned that the richest people in the world are some of the unhappiest people he's ever met.

"Drinking too much. Talking too much. Thinking too little. Retired. No purpose," he said.

To ordinary people, it sounds like an amazing life. To those who can afford to do anything, it often falls flat. Nixon elaborated:

> You feel that, gee, isn't it just great to have enough money to afford to live in a very nice house, to be able to play golf, to have nice parties, to wear good clothes, to travel if you want to?
>
> And the answer is: If you don't have those things, then they can mean a great deal to you.
>
> When you do have them, they mean nothing to you.

If you don't have those things, then they can mean a great deal to you. When you do have them, they mean nothing to you.

It's such a powerful statement. One of the most natural and common feelings with money is just chasing what you don't have.

Some people are less susceptible to this than others. But the dopamine train is such a common and powerful trap. And it helps answer the question of "What do you want out of money?" Do you want a new car? A new house? Better clothes? For most people, no, you don't actually want any of those things. At least not directly. You want everything you can't have.

Once you get them—if you do—the goalpost moves, the dopamine takes over, and you immediately begin to ask: *What's next?*

There are two big things to keep in mind here.

People often chase the wrong emotion. They go for a buzz of happiness, which is fun but fleeting. It's better to go for contentment, which feels even better and is much more durable.

If you heard the funniest joke you've ever heard, you might laugh for sixty seconds. If I told you that joke again, you might giggle a little. If I told you over and over again, you'd quickly get tired of it and ask, "Do you have any new jokes?"

Happiness is so similar. It's a wonderful feeling, but it's always fleeting. To paraphrase Don Draper: "Happiness is that feeling you get right before you need more happiness."

The problem with chasing happiness is that since it feels great but it's short-lived, you can quickly enter something that looks like an addiction cycle.

When you're content, you're no longer chasing—which is a prerequisite to being in the moment. You only get to live in the moment—enjoying what you have right now rather than dwelling on the past or dreaming about the future—when you have a complete absence of expectations that things would have or could have been better than they are now. Then you get to enjoy what you have, what you're doing, what you've created, and who you're with.

Once you view contentment as the ultimate psychological mountaintop, your goals change. You recognize that the dopamine game can never be won—there's always a next level you're striving for—and so the only way to win is to stop playing. To be content.

And let me tell you: There are few greater monetary joys than realizing that you have everything you need, right now, to be as satisfied—even as happy—as you can be.

The best measure of wealth is what you have minus what you want.

The obvious way to think of wealth is additive: You're wealthier when you have more money.

But when you realize how important expectations and contentment are, you realize the calculation is more nuanced.

The most powerful definition of wealth is not what you

have. What actually matters is the gap between what you have and what you want.

Desiring less can have the same impact on your well-being as gaining more money. But it's not only more in your control; it's a game you can actually win, leading to durable contentment instead of fleeting happiness.

And desiring less does not mean giving up. It doesn't mean you don't know how to spend money and have a good time—I think it's quite the opposite. To be content with what you have is the deepest way to enjoy the house you've purchased, the clothes you wear, and the vacations you take.

Would you rather be a billionaire who wakes up every morning anxious about what you don't have and jealous of those who have more, or an ordinary person who wakes up so content, with so much pleasure, able to appreciate what you have regardless of how much that is?

My grandmother-in-law was financially poor but psychologically rich. The gap between what she had and what she wanted was smaller than some people's with one hundred times as much money as she had.

Once you see someone master that equation, you'll never think about wealth the same.

Now let me tell you a couple stories about how having all the money in the world won't fix you if you're already miserable.

EVERYTHING YOU DON'T SEE

Happiness depends on so much more than income.
There are thirteen divorces among the ten richest
men in the world.

Would you rather make $100,000 a year with a
spouse who loves you, children who admire you,
good friends, good health, and a clear conscience,
or make $1,000,000 and have none of those things?

It's so obvious.

And now we get to an important point about money:
what it cannot do for you.

On his deathbed, former US President John Adams's last words
were "Jefferson still lives," expressing jealousy of his political
rival Thomas Jefferson. The irony is that it wasn't even true:
Unbeknownst to Adams, Jefferson had died a few hours earlier.

When you envy someone, remember that the picture you
have of their life is almost always incomplete.

As I write this, there are thirteen divorces among the ten
richest men in the world. Seven of the top ten have been di-
vorced at least once.

Correlation isn't causation, and that's a small sample size.
But a figure that is so much worse than the national aver-

age, on a topic so critical to happiness, among a group whose lives are envied by so many, is interesting, isn't it?

So much of everyone's life is invisible. Especially the difficult, depressing, and miserable parts that people try to hide. An interesting thing about money—acquiring it, having it, spending it—is that when you imagine having more of it, you focus almost exclusively on the parts of your life that might become better.

What's easy to ignore are all the hidden parts that probably won't.

There's a well-known trend with money where if you ask people, "How much money would you need to be happy?" the answer is usually about twice as much as you currently make. That's true at almost every income level—people who make $30,000 a year say they would need $60,000 to be happy, people who earn $60,000 say they would need $120,000, people who earn $1 million say they would need $2 million to feel great.

Part of the reason this occurs is because it's easy to view having more money as the tonic for all your ills. When you realize it's not, the tendency is to assume that, well, if you just had a little more, that would do the trick. This focus on what more money could do, while ignoring what it can't, can trap people on a psychological treadmill.

————

J. Paul Getty was once the richest man in the world, one of the first people to accumulate more than $1 billion. In a 1963 documentary, Getty was interviewed at his seven-hundred-acre, seventy-two-room Sutton Place castle. It is one of the more ornate and over-the-top homes to ever exist. Getty is asked, over and over, what it's like to live like a modern king. His answers are mostly shrugs—it becomes clear that for all the money in the world, this is not a man bubbling with joy. Finally, Getty is asked who he envies. He says:

> I envy people younger and stronger and more cheerful than I am, people who have better characters than I have . . . I always wished that I had a better personality, that I could entertain people better. I always worried I might be a little on the dull side.

It's a fascinating answer, because you might expect him to say that he envies his competitors, or people from a different era who were more successful. But the people he actually envies could have been infinitely poorer and less successful than he was. If you're already miserable, having more money might not do much for you. That can be so hard for people striving for more money to accept. And yet.

Most of what makes you happy in life has nothing to do with money, and realizing that once you have money can be a painful admission.

Will Smith wrote in his biography that when he was poor and depressed, he could dream about a future when he had more money, and that money making his problems go away. Once he was rich, that optimism was gone. He had all the money he could ever need and he was still depressed, his life was still filled with problems.

Music executive Rick Rubin once echoed something similar:

> It's hard to get really depressed until your dreams come true. Once your dreams come true and you realize you feel the same way you did before, then you get a feeling of hopelessness.

He later elaborated:

> I think we mistakenly think that some kind of outward success is going to change something in us. And it does not. It may make life more comfortable. But it doesn't change who we are. And any hole in ourselves that we're hoping to fill does not get filled.
>
> And let's say you spend 20 years of your life working towards something that's going to solve everything, and then you finally achieve what you've been trying to do for 20 years, toiling away . . . and nothing changes. That's when you get hopeless.

This happens so often when people meet some financial goal, or buy a new toy. What you thought would change your life and turn you into a walking ball of happiness very likely does not, which can be agonizing to experience.

Happiness is complicated, but if you simplify it into things like a loving family, health, friendship, eight hours of sleep, well-balanced children, and being part of something bigger than yourself, you realize how limited money's role can be. It's not that it has no role, just smaller than you may have assumed.

Of course, you can be poor and miserable or rich and happy. But only those who have gained significant wealth are aware of how tenuous that relationship can be. Gaining money probably didn't fix your marriage, it didn't make you more attractive, it didn't make your friends like you more, it didn't make you more fulfilled—at least as much as you assumed. So what used to be comforting optimism about what money could do for you is replaced by the stark reality of what it can't. Sometimes the dream is what feels good, and once you've hit it the dream is gone and you actually become depressed. Malcolm Forbes said: "By the time we've made it, we've had it."

———

My wife and I used to live in Southern California. Then we lived in Washington, DC. Hardly a day went by in DC that we didn't miss California's weather. Los Angeles is seventy degrees in the winter and eighty degrees in the summer. The East Coast has two temperatures: repulsively hot and inhumanely cold.

Here's what's hard to come to terms with: We missed California's weather because we thought it would make us happier. But there's no evidence, either for us or anyone else, that Californians are happier than their East Coast counterparts. The happiest states in America are the Dakotas, Nebraska, and Minnesota—home to some of the most insulting climates in this hemisphere.

Money can be so similar.

The late psychologist Daniel Kahneman once said, "Nothing in life is as important as you think it is when you are thinking about it." He pointed out that "paraplegics are often unhappy, but they are not unhappy all the time, because they spend most of the time experiencing and thinking about things other than their disability." In the same way, those with tons of money might be often happy, but they are not happy all the time, because they spend most of the time experiencing and thinking about things other than their money. Here's Kahneman again (emphasis mine):

> On average, individuals with high incomes are in a better mood than people with lower income, but the difference is about a third as large as most people expect. **When you think of rich and poor people, your thoughts are inevitably focused on circumstances in which income is important. But happiness depends on other factors more than it depends on income.**

It is easy, for example, to imagine having more money and think that a bigger house will make you happy. You imagine the giant living room, the marble bathroom, the curved staircase. In that specific context, it seems amazing—and maybe it is. What's easy to ignore—the part you don't see or pay attention to—are things like how hard it is to clean, six-figure bills to replace something mundane like gutters, neighbors who sue you because they don't like your land-scaping because that's the kind of thing rich neighbors do, and so on endlessly. You also think about enjoying your big backyard in a vacuum, isolated from the reality that people with big backyards still have indigestion, seasonal allergies, and the flu as much as their less-affluent peers. You ignore that people with big backyards also get angry at their co-workers and have jerk bosses and annoying clients. You ca-sually disregard that people with in-home theaters argue with their spouses and compare themselves to their more success-ful peers as much as anyone else.

All of those things subtract from the bliss we imagine ourselves in when dreaming about having and spending more money. When it's easy and fun to think about the up-side of what more money can provide you, but equally easy to ignore what won't change or what baggage comes along with having more stuff, you get disappointment.

None of this is to say that money can't make you happier. It's just less of a miracle drug than we often assume. And when it does make you happier, it's often for nuanced rea-sons. A few key things to keep in mind here:

If you're already an unhappy person, it's unlikely that more money will ever fix your problems.

Matthew Killingsworth from the University of Pennsylvania settled decades of debate in academic circles about the relationship between money and happiness—some studies had shown there's a clear correlation between the two, others didn't.

When he drilled down into the data, people who were already rated as having low emotional well-being saw no improvement in happiness when their incomes rose above $100,000 a year. For the middle group of emotional well-being, happiness tended to improve with extra income. For people who were already super happy, making more money was like a happiness accelerant.

"If you're rich and miserable, more money won't help," Killingsworth wrote.

So many factors go into happiness that having more money can be a drop in the bucket amid a tsunami of other things that create an unhappy life.

A related point is that the core ingredients that truly make people happy—friends, family, health, meaning, a clear mind—cannot be purchased, only earned.

When spending more money does make you happier, it's usually for indirect reasons.

Spending money on a nice, big house might make me happier—but probably because it makes it easier to entertain friends and family, and spending time with those people is actually what makes me happier. It's the same with vacations—going to Maui might be a joy, but perhaps the best part is a week of uninterrupted, work-free, email-free, commute-free time with your family.

You can look at this from the opposite direction: Will a big, nice house make you happy if you don't have friends and family to share it with? Will the vacation make you happy if you don't enjoy spending time with your family? Will a fancy car make you happy if you only drive it while commuting to a job you despise?

If you already have some of the core ingredients for happiness, spending money can be like leverage for a good life. But if you're lacking in some of those core areas, it becomes a false crutch. And it's a frustrating one, because we're so hardwired to think that having more money and spending more money should always lead to a better life.

Never focus on what money can do for you without a clear understanding of the cost of acquiring more of it.

Taylor Swift, remembering her drive early in her career, once said, "I would think about exactly how I was going to get there—not just how it would feel to be there."

That's rare. It's so much easier to fantasize about the trophy while ignoring the stress of the race. If I dream about how much better my life will be if I could spend more money, there's a good chance I'm dismissing the potential costs of acquiring that money—stressful jobs, long hours, uncertainty, time away from doing other things I enjoy.

It's an important example of what you are often blind to with money. Another successful entertainer, Jimmy Carr, says, "Everyone is jealous of what you've got, no one is jealous of how you got it."

So much of a good life is about what didn't happen.

It's the fights you didn't have, the illnesses you avoided, and the unhealthy desires you didn't feed. It's the unaffordable lifestyle you didn't choose to live, the mistakes you didn't make, and the regrets you don't have.

In truth, I can probably see 1 percent of what's important in your life, and you can see 1 percent of mine. If that. When so much of a good life is not just hidden but things that never happened, we focus too much on what's visible and easy to measure—people's homes, cars, clothes, jewelry, vacations, and toys—and overestimate their importance.

Looking back, whether you lived a good life will likely have little to do with how much money you made or spent.

Marc Randolph, cofounder of Netflix, once wrote this beautiful note:

> I resolved a long time ago to not be one of those
> entrepreneurs on their 7th startup and their
> 7th wife. In fact, the thing I'm most proud of in
> my life is not the companies I started, it's the

fact that I was able to start them while staying married to the same woman; having my kids grow up knowing me and (best as I can tell) liking me, and being able to spend time pursuing the other passions in my life.

That's my definition of success.

It's a wonderful philosophy. What matters more than the money you make and the money you spend is the less tangible parts of life that can't be purchased.

Next, an astounding and tragic story of two men who chose opposite lifestyles, and what they can teach us about internal versus external benchmarks.

THE MOST VALUABLE FINANCIAL ASSET IS NOT NEEDING TO IMPRESS ANYONE

The ability to not need to prove yourself to strangers is priceless.

N ot needing to impress other people, especially strangers, is an asset on your personal balance sheet that can be more valuable than anything else.

When you don't feel the need to impress other people, your desires fall. When your desires fall, your satisfaction with what you already have grows. It's really that simple.

There are always two benchmarks to measure yourself against to determine how well you're doing in life: internal and external. The first is how happy you are with yourself, the other is what other people think of you.

It's astounding to watch how agonizing it can be when someone focuses too much on the external benchmark. And it's so thrilling to witness someone whose only goal in life is to nail their internal benchmarks.

Let me tell you an extreme story of two guys on opposite ends of that spectrum. Their stories have nothing to do with money but can teach us so much about how important it is to pick the right benchmark in life.

In 1968 the *Sunday Times* newspaper in London, looking to drum up some publicity and capitalize on the growing sport of sailing, sponsored an around-the-world boat race. The goal was simple: The first person to sail around the world nonstop, solo, would win the Golden Globe Race.

It was called a race, but that was technically an afterthought: No one in human history had ever sailed around the world solo nonstop. So the first person to merely complete the task would instantly be crowned one of the greatest sailors in history.

There were no qualification requirements and few rules. Nine men joined the race, one of whom had never sailed. Just one man finished, almost one year and twenty-seven thousand miles later.

But it was two of the sailors who did not finish who had the most remarkable voyages and stunned the world—for opposite reasons.

The two men—Donald Crowhurst and Bernard Moitessier—are incredible examples of how the quality of your life is shaped by who you want to impress. Their stories are wild and extreme, but what they dealt with was just a magnified version of what ordinary people face all the time.

Donald Crowhurst once said life was a game only the clever would win. To him, cleverness was the most valuable trait, and lying was OK if it made people happy and helped you win the game. Both ideas would eventually come back to haunt him.

Born in 1932, Crowhurst was thirty-six years old when he first heard of the Golden Globe Race. There are two important things to know about his life up until this point:

Despite huge ambition, he had been a professional failure at nearly everything he had tried. He was kicked out of both the Royal Air Force and the British Army before starting a business that never took off and was on the brink of failure. He viewed the Golden Globe as a new shot at redemption, a chance to finally show the world he was worthy of attention.

He was not a very good sailor. At best Crowhurst was a weekend sailor, taking his boat out for short trips while being prone to seasickness.

But rarely short of confidence, Crowhurst was convinced his homemade sailing navigation equipment could not only propel him to win the *Sunday Times* race, but that doing so would generate enough attention to save his business.

He faced just a few obstacles: He didn't own a boat, he was broke, and he stood no chance of financing the race himself.

Crowhurst struck a deal with an English businessman named Stanley Best who agreed to cover the cost of equipment for the race under two conditions: They would orchestrate a media frenzy, portraying Crowhurst as a sailing savant. And if Crowhurst failed to finish, he would owe all the money back.

While preparing for the race, the BBC was enamored with Crowhurst—the brave, unknown amateur about to undertake the hardest race in sailing history. You have to understand how insane this race was. The most grizzled sailors in the world thought it nearly impossible to sail around the world solo nonstop. Now here was Crowhurst, a man the sailing community had never heard of, with almost no experience, stepping up. He reveled in the attention.

"The thing about Donald was that he thought himself God," one of Crowhurst's friends said.

But he wasn't, and the day before Crowhurst set sail around the globe he realized how woefully unprepared he was. His boat, the *Teignmouth Electron*, had been so heavily modified, so weighed down with half-finished gizmos and gimmicks, that it was barely seaworthy for a short sail near home, let alone a solo trip around the globe.

Crowhurst's wife, Clare, tried talking him out of the race. "I suppose you're right," he said, "but the whole thing has become too important for me. I've got to go through with it."

After a long pause, he continued: "Darling, I'm very disappointed in the boat. She's not right. I'm not prepared. If I leave with things in this hopeless state will you go out of your mind with worry?"

Clare responded with a question: "If you give up now, will you be unhappy for the rest of your life?"

Donald offered no response and began to cry.

Prepared or not, Crowhurst set sail from Teignmouth, England, on October 31, 1968.

It was a disappointment from the start. After two weeks at sea, Crowhurst had covered less than half the distance he intended.

Then disaster: Crowhurst's boat began to leak. "This bloody boat is just falling to pieces due to lack of attention to engineering detail," he wrote in his diary.

The boat was not at risk of sinking, but the incoming water fried its electronics and generator, all but ending any chance of finishing the race. Worse, if Crowhurst continued to the rough seas of the South Atlantic, he knew his fragile boat could quickly capsize.

"What courses are open? Either I abandon the non-stop attempt or I go on with it. If I go on I have an equal chance of making the trip or drowning," he wrote in his diary.

The alternative might be worse. If Crowhurst turned around and went home, he would face not only bankruptcy after being forced to repay the borrowed funds, but shame and humiliation for failing at yet another endeavor.

Then the clever Crowhurst realized there was a third option, which was outright fraud and deceit.

Crowhurst began loitering in the Atlantic, drifting aimlessly in circles in calm water. He then began sending fake coordinates back to England, giving the impression that he was still sailing around the world.

The plan was simple: If Crowhurst could kill enough time drifting in the Atlantic—likely six months or more—he could convince people that he had plausibly sailed around the world before returning to England with his dignity intact.

At this point in the race Crowhurst began keeping two logbooks: one with his fake locations, which he plotted by reverse engineering how fast he could plausibly have made it to an imaginary destination, and one with his actual location. Tracking his actual location was vital to ensure he remained where he was unlikely to be spotted by other boats, whose crews might reveal his position to the press back home.

You need to be an utter genius to pull off a fraud like this. Crowhurst was not. In the first few days of hatching his scheme, he made his first major error. While reporting his fake coordinates to the race organizers back home, Crowhurst's sloppy calculations gave the impression he was suddenly moving at blistering speed, covering an unprecedented amount of distance.

The press, having no idea of what was actually happening, ate it up. *The Sunday Times* wrote:

> Donald Crowhurst, last man out in the Sunday Times round-the-world lone-man yacht race, covered a breathtaking and possibly record-breaking 243 miles in his 41 foot trimaran Teignmouth Electron last Sunday. The achievement is even more remarkable in the light of the very poor speeds in the first three weeks of his voyage; he took longer to reach the Cape Verdes than any other competitor. In his last radio message Crowhurst said he was on watch for the full 24 hours. "It took a pretty strong nerve. I have never sailed so fast in my life."

It was all a lie.

It went on like this for months—Crowhurst drifting

around the Atlantic, depressed and scared, sending fake co-ordinates back to the race organizers, while everyone at home thought he was pulling off the most heroic feat in sailing history.

As he plotted his eventual return home, Crowhurst realized he did not want to win the race—doing so would spark so much attention that the sailing community might dig through his logbooks and discover the deceit. Coming in second place seemed ideal: an incredible performance that would make him a hero, but not so famous that experts would examine his voyage too deeply.

Crowhurst knew another sailor, Nigel Tetley, was on track to win the fastest time around the world. Crowhurst strategically inserted himself into second place but made another error, coming too close to Tetley. Tetley became nervous about a competitor hot on his tail and began pushing his sailboat harder and harder, past the limits that it could handle. While desperately trying to gain distance on Crowhurst, Tetley's boat fell to pieces and sank in the Atlantic (he survived on his life raft).

Crowhurst was now on track to win the Golden Globe Race and be crowned the greatest sailor of all time.

Supporters at home were stunned.

On June 18 the BBC sent Crowhurst a telegram that read:

CONGRATULATIONS ON PROGRESS

HAVE NETWORK TELEVISION PROGRAMME

FOR DAY OF RETURN

In the town of Teignmouth, a "Welcome Home Donald Crowhurst" committee was formed to celebrate its new hero. The plan was for a BBC helicopter to follow him back to port while a parade, complete with a firing cannon, met his triumphant return.

Crowhurst's diary makes clear how much this impending fame—all of it ill-gotten, all of it risky if the truth was uncovered—worried him.

Life was a game to Crowhurst. As he pondered his fate, he wrote in his diary: "Cannot see any 'purpose' in game . . . I am what I am and I see the nature of my offence."

Then came more ominous entries. One read:

It is finished
It is finished
It is the mercy

And the final entry:

It is the end of my game. The truth has been revealed and it will be done as my family require me to do it . . . I have no need to prolong the game. It has been a good game must be ended . . . I will play this game when I choose I will resign the game . . .

The *Teignmouth Electron* was found eleven days later, adrift in the Atlantic. There was no sign of major damage, no sign of any accident—and no sign of Donald Crowhurst.

He was never seen again. He had, in all likelihood, thrown himself into the sea and taken his own life.

In a sweet twist of irony, Robin Knox-Johnston, the only man to finish the Golden Globe Race, donated the £5,000 in prize money to Clare Crowhurst. It was enough to spare her the bankruptcy that Donald Crowhurst dreaded would haunt his family if he didn't finish the race.

Just before Crowhurst took his life, another sailor in the Golden Globe Race made an equally astonishing decision at sea.

Bernard Moitessier *was* an expert sailor, and five months into the race, he was on track to *legitimately* win.

Moitessier—a Frenchman who was forty-eight years old during the race—loved sailing, and spent most of his life at sea. But he seemed to despise the commercialization of his sport. The idea of performing for the media, the sponsors, the press, seemed to damage his soul. He just liked sailing for sailing's sake.

Moitessier didn't even bring a radio on his trip, preferring solitude and letting other passing ships report his location to the race organizers back in England. The personality required to spend nine months alone at sea selects people who are comfortable detaching from society. Moitessier was an extreme version of that, and the idea of sailing for someone else's pleasure was so detestable that midway through his voyage he'd had enough.

He wrote in his diary:

> I really felt sick at the thought of getting back to Europe, back to the snakepit . . . I am really fed up with false gods, always lying in wait, spider-like, eating our liver, sucking our marrow. I charge the modern world—that's the Monster, trampling the soul of men.

But being on his boat, *Joshua*, was a different story. That actually fed his soul. Moitessier later recalled:

> The days go by, never monotonous. Even when they appear exactly alike they are never quite the same. That is what gives life at sea its special dimension, made up of contemplation and very simple contrasts. Sea, winds, calms, sun, clouds, porpoises. Peace, and the joy of being alive in harmony.

As he sailed around Cape Horn on his way back to England, Moitessier began contemplating the unthinkable: quitting the race he was on track to win and sailing somewhere else.

Thinking of his family and friends, he wrote:

> I do not know how to explain to them my need to be at peace, to continue toward the Pacific. They will not understand. I know I'm right, I feel it deeply. I know exactly where I am going, even if I do not know.

Then he made his decision.

Moitessier flagged down a passing commercial ship to hand off a message. It was a letter addressed to the editor of *The Sunday Times* that read:

Dear Robert, today is March 18th. I am continuing non-stop toward the Pacific Islands because I am happy at sea, and perhaps to save my soul.

Moitessier shouted for the captain to take the message to the French consul.

He then quit the race, turned his boat around, and set sail for Tahiti.

Moitessier wrote in his diary:

Now it is a story between *Joshua* and me, between me and the sky; a story just for us, a great story that does not concern the others any more . . . To have the time, to have the choice, not knowing what you are heading for and just going there anyway, without a care, without asking any more questions.

To some at home, Moitessier had gone mad. In his mind, he had found his own version of sanity.

He anchored in Tahiti in June, built a house on the beach, grew his own food, and wrote a book about sailing.

"You can't understand how happy I am," he wrote.

In a twist of irony, Tahiti was so far out of the way and

required so much backtracking that, despite dropping out of the race, Moitessier did circle the globe, and set a world record for the longest ever nonstop solo sail—more than thirty-seven thousand miles.

There is no mention of that fact in his book. He didn't seem to care whether anyone else knew, and certainly didn't want the attention.

The point of this story is not to ridicule Crowhurst or heroize Moitessier. Nine months alone at sea is enough to drive anyone mad. I can sympathize with Crowhurst's feelings of desperation. And Moitessier's decision, though perhaps right for him, would be disastrous for most people, who enjoy, if not crave, social acceptance.

But extreme examples often highlight emotions many people experience every day, and I think that's the case here.

It's very simple: Crowhurst was addicted to what other people thought of his accomplishments, while Moitessier could not have cared less. One lived for external benchmarks, the other only cared about internal measures of happiness.

And knowing the difference between the two is so, so powerful in life.

Warren Buffett once said: "The big question about how people behave is whether they've got an Inner Scorecard or an Outer Scorecard. It helps if you can be satisfied with an Inner Scorecard."

He used this example: Would you rather be known as the best investor in the world but in reality be the worst, or be thought of as the world's worst investor when you were actually the best?

That's another extreme example, but it gets you thinking about what actually matters to you.

Every decision we make when spending money falls into one of two buckets: Are you spending money on something because it makes people think differently of you—like you more, be more impressed with you, maybe even jealous of you—or because it actually feeds your soul and makes you happy?

Using Buffett's framework: Would you rather people be impressed with your possessions but be miserable inside, or have no one care what you own but wake up happy every morning?

I have no idea how to find the perfect balance between internal and external benchmarks. But I know there's a strong social pull toward external measures—chasing a path someone else set, whether you enjoy it or not. Social media makes it ten times more powerful.

But I also know there's a strong natural desire for internal measures—being independent, following your quirky habits, and doing what you want, when you want, with whom you want.

That's money's highest purpose, because that's what most people *actually* want.

Next, an important twist on this idea, with the story of a blind man who can teach us so much about happiness.

WHAT MAKES YOU HAPPY

A good life is everything you need and some of what you want. If you have everything you want, you appreciate none of what you have.

M ichael May suffered a horrific accident when he was a baby that left him completely blind. A miraculous surgery restored his vision at age forty-six when, from his perspective, he could see the world for the first time in his life.

As May left the doctor's office after his successful surgery, he walked through the lobby and one thing stopped him in his tracks: the carpet. The standard, drab office carpet.

"Look at those shapes! Look at those colors!" he excitedly told his wife. It was the most beautiful thing his mind could ever imagine.

As he looked around the lobby, he saw other patients waiting for their appointments. He couldn't fathom why none of them were freaking out about the carpet. Didn't they see what he saw? May's biographer, Robert Kurson, writes: "He could not believe they were just sitting there ignoring this carpet—how could a person just sit there when such a carpet was happening?"

At one point May stops and mumbles, "That's blue. Oh my gosh, that's blue." He had dreamed what colors might look like but his mind could never quite understand it, until now.

As he moves through the office, he does the same thing with wall paintings, exit signs, and—the most stunning of all—seeing numbers on a piece of paper for the first time ever.

It was all so beautiful, so overwhelming to him. Because he had never seen anything before, May was getting probably ten thousand times more pleasure and awe looking at an office carpet than you and I would from viewing the most perfect, radiant sunset.

Isn't there so much to learn from that? The most mundane things can feel incredible when they're a contrast to what you're used to.

A weird thing is that everyone strives for a good life because they think it will make them happy. But what actually brings happiness is the contrast between what you have now and whatever you were just experiencing.

The best drink you will ever taste is a glass of tap water when you're thirsty.

The best meal you will ever eat is cheap food when you're starving.

The best sleep you will ever experience is when your newborn allows you to sneak in a quick nap.

There is no such thing as an objectively good experience—every amount of "good" is just the gap between expectations and reality. It's the distance between what you have now and what you either had or expected before. The contrast, not the amount, is what makes you happy.

Few things are as important to keep in mind while spending money.

A good life is everything you need and some of what you want. If you have everything you want, you appreciate none of what you have.

William Dawson once wrote:

> The thing that is least perceived about wealth is that all pleasure in money ends at the point where economy becomes unnecessary. The man who can buy anything he covets, without any consultation with his banker, values nothing that he buys.

The anticipation of something you're saving up for, the surprise of getting something you didn't expect, the change in circumstances from one period to the next, is what makes certain purchases feel valuable.

Consider how you felt when you got your first paycheck from your first job. If you celebrated with as little as a cheap milkshake, you probably had a joyous feeling of *I did this. I bought this. With my own money.* Going from not being able to buy anything to being able to buy something is an amazing feeling.

The gap between struggle and reward is a big part of what makes people happy.

Contrast that with later in your career, when (hopefully) savings have been built and paychecks have grown. It's not that spending won't make you happy—but it won't be as thrilling and adrenaline-inducing as it was when there was more struggle and contrast behind each dollar. The richest you'll probably ever feel is when you get your first paycheck and your bank account goes from $5 to, perhaps, $500. The contrast that generates might be greater than going from $10 million to $20 million. Going from nothing to something can be so much more powerful than going from a lot to even more.

Contrast, contrast, contrast. Once you see how powerful it is, you appreciate how important it is.

I know a guy with a private chef. He's served five-star meals three times a day, an arrangement he's enjoyed for years. It's amazing; I'd lie if I said I wasn't jealous. But I also wonder if the joy diminishes over time. He doesn't have to struggle to get these meals—there's no anticipation, no looking forward to a rare restaurant reservation, no contrasting gap between a "normal" meal and his daily delicacy. Does he get more pleasure out of his third five-star meal of the day than a child gets when a parent offers a surprise trip to McDonald's and the kid savors the first bite? I doubt it.

So much of being happy with your money is battling the hedonic treadmill—the ability to become accustomed to something you once considered a luxury. One way to fight back is respecting the idea that occasional treats can generate more joy than perpetual luxury.

Arnold Schwarzenegger once gave diet advice: "You should mostly eat food you know is healthy. . . . You should also occasionally let yourself eat delicious food you know isn't healthy. Otherwise what's the point?"

What's the point? So much of the reason you do the right thing is because it makes occasionally doing the wrong thing (responsibly) feel so much better.

There's a financial version of this that's tied to the previous chapter and the idea of contentment. When you're content with what you have now, an occasional treat or surprise can feel incredible. It's a surprise, it's a joy. You appreciate and savor it more. And the more content you are now, the more frequently you'll stumble across little things in life that feel like a treat—a surprise dinner, a hotel room upgrade, a rare splurge, even if it's small. When you expect nothing, everything is a surprise. When everything is a surprise, you walk around like Michael May, ecstatic over the littlest things you'd otherwise take for granted.

Everyone's different, but my own desire to live a relatively simple life is not because I don't enjoy nice things. It's quite the opposite. When you live a simple and modest life, your occasional experience with nice things can generate more joy than if you had those things all the time.

I'm not recommending you deprive yourself of something you want, can afford, and that makes you happy. I'm merely pointing out how much influence your expectations have on your well-being. People struggle through grueling hours of work they often don't enjoy for a chance at buying stuff they assume will make them happier. It feels like such an obvious thing to do. It's much harder to recognize that there's often more psychological upside to managing your expectations down rather than attempting to push your circumstances up. The reason is not just because you learn to be happy with less, but because the occasional treat becomes that much more delightful.

Christmas morning, the Fourth of July, birthdays, and the last day of school feel great because they happen just once a year. The same joy can be had when the luxury items in your life become occasional treats rather than constant needs.

———

Ernest Shackleton's ship, the *Endurance*, became stuck in Antarctic ice. Before long, it was crushed, ruined.

Shackleton and his twenty-seven-man crew then spent nineteen months—from January 1915 to August 1916—rowing eight hundred miles to safety in tiny lifeboats, with nighttime temperatures hitting ten degrees below zero.

They were constantly freezing, wet, hungry, and sleep-deprived. They survived—and all of them *did* survive—on an occasionally captured seal and foraged seaweed. It's one of the most astounding survival stories you'll ever hear.

But, for me, the most emotional part of the story comes at the end, when Shackleton's crew finally made it to a whaling station on South Georgia island, sixteen hundred miles east of Argentina, where they received aid. Author Alfred Lansing writes:

> Every comfort the whaling station could provide was placed at the disposal of Shackleton [and crew]. They first enjoyed the glorious lux-

ury of a long bath, followed by a shave. Then new clothes were given to them from the station's storehouse.

They were then served a hot meal, and slept for twelve hours.

Can you even imagine what that must have felt like?

Can you imagine how good it must have felt to have a bath, a hot meal, and a warm bed after being constantly frozen and starving for nineteen months?

Even if the water was lukewarm and the food was half-stale, that must have been one of the most pleasant and fulfilling evenings anyone has ever experienced.

It's a strange feeling to read these stories. I would never want to experience the hardship they, or Michael May, endured. But I am a little jealous of the overwhelming joy they must have experienced when their hardship was over.

It's the same with money. I don't want to live a life of destitution, deprived of all luxury. But I have an even stronger desire to experience the joy that contrast delivers when I experience an occasional luxury, a nice surprise, an unexpected treat.

A few things I keep in mind here:

A simple life can be the most potent way to enjoy luxury items.

That's so counterintuitive until you realize how powerful contrast can be. Figure out your own details, everyone's different, but when I find something I love—a restaurant, a trip, a drink—I tend to ask how I can turn it into an occasional treat versus a constant new addition.

When you are content with a simple life, the occasional treat truly feels like magic.

The power of contrast can make ordinary things feel incredible and extraordinary things feel bland.

Rich people who fly in their own private jets will tell you it's the most amazing, satisfying thing extreme wealth can buy, and it never gets old. Why don't we ordinary people say the same thing about driving in our own cars—"private cars"? My theory is that most people who fly in private jets used to fly commercial before they were rich, so they remember the slog of flying like an ordinary person: long lines, going through security, the middle seat, the snoring passengers. Compared to that, flying private is a dream.

But most people who drive "private" cars don't have anything similar to compare the experience with. They've been in "private" cars their whole life. There is no contrast between current and previous experiences.

But go back to the early 1900s, when cars *were* new and people could contrast the experience to the horse and buggy. What did people say about cars back then? They seemed so magical and luxurious that many feared they would create a haves-versus-have-nots war that could tear the country apart. In 1906 Woodrow Wilson, who was then president of Princeton University, said, "Nothing has spread socialistic feeling in this country more than the automobile," and that it offered "a picture of the arrogance of wealth." Exactly as people talk about private jets today.

When you have no contrast against current experiences, amazing things can feel completely ordinary.

When you realize how powerful expectations are, you put as much effort into keeping them low as you do into improving your circumstances.

Happiness, contentment, joy . . . all of those things come from experiencing a gap between expectations and reality.

Shackleton's men learned this. After their ordeal, they found so much joy in little things they'd never before considered. One crew member wrote in his diary as they reached land: "One of the finest days we have ever had . . . a pleasure to be alive."

Lansing wrote: "In this lonely world of ice and emptiness, they had achieved at least a limited kind of contentment. They had been tested and found not wanting."

That's about as good as it gets.

THE RICH AND THE WEALTHY

Being controlled by money is a hidden form of debt.
And like all debt, it will eventually be repaid plus
interest.

L et me make a distinction between rich and wealthy.
The definitions are my own, but I've always found them helpful.

If you are rich, you have money in the bank that allows you to buy the stuff you want.

If you are wealthy, you have a level of control over what that money does to your personality, your freedom, your desires, ambitions, morals, friendships, and mental health.

When figuring out how to spend money in a way that will make you happy, I've found that it's not so much about how much money you have or how much you spend. The trick is whether you are—or aspire to be—this definition of rich or wealthy.

Money is a powerful tool, capable of shaping people's lives in extraordinary ways.

That statement can either be an inspiration or a curse, because here's the truth: If you don't figure out how to use money correctly, *it will use you.*

It will control you. It will make you its prisoner, showing no mercy and offering no sympathy.

Some people are so controlled by money that they think they're chasing money to live a better life, but in fact the money plays them like a marionette doll, pulling the strings and demanding that they chase things they may not like and aspire to things they don't even understand.

If I asked, "Is it a good thing to be obsessed with drugs, or alcohol, or fame, or power?" you would say of course not—obsession with almost *anything* can turn into a liability, because it begins to control you. What you intended to be a helpful tool becomes a controlling dictator.

A dangerous obsession with money—particularly spending money—can creep into your life unnoticed, because the allure of what money can do for you is so enchanting. The idea that you will be happier if you just had more money to spend is so powerful and so universal that people have a hard time distinguishing noble ambition from dangerous obsession.

Being controlled by money can apply to everyone, at every income level. But you see its power under a magnifying glass among the very rich, who are blessed with lots of money but often cursed by the control it has on their lives.

It can be a shocking thing to witness, throwing you off guard when you realize that someone who has so much money has lost so much control over their life. Ernest Hemingway said fellow author F. Scott Fitzgerald had a "romantic awe of [the rich]. . . . He thought they were a special glamorous race and when he found they weren't it wrecked him as much as any other thing that wrecked him."

Let me share a story of one of the richest families in human history, who were so obsessed with spending money that it led to a life I find more pitiful than enviable.

Reginald Claypoole Vanderbilt was born into a family fractured by bitter rivalries, fragile egos, and insurmountable expectations. Everything went downhill from there.

When Reggie's great-grandfather, Cornelius "Commodore" Vanderbilt, died in 1877, the *New York Daily Tribune* published an editorial predicting the legacy of the world's richest man:

> The Vanderbilt case is an impressive lesson in the folly of attempting to "found a family" upon no better basis than the possession of money.
>
> The ruling idea of the Old Commodore's latter years was to amass a huge fortune which should stand for generations as a monument to the name of Vanderbilt, and make the head of the house a permanent power in American society.
>
> There is no country in the world where fortunes are made so quickly . . . and none in which inherited money has done so little for its possessors.

The Vanderbilt money is certainly bringing no happiness and no greatness to its present claimants, and we have little doubt that in the course of a few years, it will go the way of most American fortunes; a multitude of heirs will have the spending of it, and it will be absorbed in the vast circulating system of the country.

It was a brutal outlook—and underestimated what was to come.

Adjusted for inflation, Cornelius Vanderbilt left his heirs something like $300 billion. He allegedly had more money than the US Treasury. Within sixty years almost nothing was left.

The wealth went to three generations whose guiding life purpose was to see who could spend it the fastest and most recklessly. Early heirs felt some duty to run the family business; over time the "family business" became insecurity and resentment.

In 1875 an op-ed said socialites "devote themselves to pleasure regardless of expense." A Vanderbilt quipped that actually they "devote themselves to expense regardless of pleasure."

That frank admission was really the heart of it. It was a game that couldn't be won, so everyone lost.

Being controlled by money is a hidden form of debt. And like all debt, it will eventually be repaid at significant cost.

Reggie was one of the last Vanderbilt heirs to inherit significant wealth. On his twenty-first birthday he inherited $12.5 million, or about $350 million in today's dollars.

Family biographer Arthur Vanderbilt writes:

> Self-indulgent, lazy, lackadaisical, Reggie had ab-
> solutely no sense of responsibility or purpose
> other than to keep himself from being bored . . .
> [he was] never employed and never did a lick of
> work. Somewhat at a loss when asked his occupa-
> tion, he usually responded, 'Gentleman.' . . . The
> only way Reggie could distinguish himself was
> to live the life of a rich playboy. And this he did
> with dedication and consummate skill.

Reggie's two great loves were liquor and gambling. The first left him dead at age forty-five, with cirrhosis so severe the blood flow from his liver was choked off and pushed up to his esophagus, where veins abruptly ruptured and left him choking in a pool of blood as his family watched in horror. The latter left him broke—after debts were repaid, Reggie's will was nearly irrelevant, since he had nowhere near the amount of money promised to his heirs.

The Vanderbilts had the biggest homes, the most glorious furnishings, the most extravagant parties, and the most exquisite travel. But so much of it was purchased as a monument to their wealth—virtually worshipping it like a deity—rather than using it as a tool that could improve their lives. The result was something between absurdity and tragedy.

While Reggie's life was spinning out of control, another Vanderbilt heir, George Washington Vanderbilt, spent six years building the 135,000-square-foot Biltmore house—with forty master bedrooms and a full-time staff of nearly four hundred. He allegedly spent little time there because it felt more like a commercial building than a cozy home—it was "utterly unaddressed to any possible arrangement of life," as one friend put it. The house nevertheless cost so much to maintain it nearly ruined Vanderbilt. Ninety percent of the land was sold off to pay tax debts, and the house was turned into a tourist attraction.

Then there were family rivalries over who could build the biggest yacht, buy the most expensive art, or marry the bluest blood. The rivalry—not the material pleasure—was the point, which ensured happiness was always out of reach. There were arranged marriages, endless bitter disputes over inheritance, and almost never a chance for heirs to find their own way or be known as anything other than a trust-funder.

Just before he died in 1920, William Vanderbilt said, "My life was never destined to be quite happy. Inherited wealth is a real handicap to happiness. It is as a death to ambition as cocaine is to morality."

At almost every turn, money tore the family apart, leading to a level of dysfunction and insecurity you would not wish upon your enemies.

Dig into the lives of the Vanderbilt heirs—history's luckiest members of the lucky sperm club—and not many of you would want to swap lives. You look at this enormous wealth that tore the family apart and you begin to ask, "What was the point?"

The point, as the *New York Daily Tribune* realized early on, was not to live a great life. It was not to use their money as a tool to become happier, more content, more enriched, or more satisfied. The point was just to be rich and to spend—to be valued "upon no better basis than the possession of money."

Rather than using money to build a life, their life was built around money; rather than an asset, their inheritance functioned as an insurmountable lifestyle debt, passed to the next generation until there was mercifully nothing left.

It's hard to have sympathy for billionaire heirs. But the important part here is diagnosing the problem, because it's one that afflicts many ordinary people: The Vanderbilts are one of the clearest examples of money controlling a person, rather than being used as a tool to improve their life. They lived to serve their money, rather than the other way around.

It's not an isolated example. Entrepreneur David Siegel once built a 90,000-square-foot house in Florida. Asked why he was building such a big house, he thought about it for a moment and replied: "Because I can." To each their own, but he said nothing about the memories it would enhance or the pleasure it would bring—just "Because I can." That, to me, smells like someone whose money has complete control over their personality. (Back to the tool: If someone asked why you're using a screwdriver, you would not say, "Because I can." You would say, "Because it helps me hang pictures on the wall and put furniture together." The master-versus-tool framework is so powerful once you look for it.)

Harvey Firestone, the late tire tycoon, seemed to fall for this same trap. To his credit, he was aware of the silly game his money made him play. He wrote in his 1926 memoir:

> Why is it that a man, just as soon as he gets enough money, builds a house much bigger than he needs?
>
> I have a house in Akron many times larger than I have the least use for; I have another house at Miami Beach which is also much larger than I need. I suppose that before I die I shall buy or build other houses which also will be larger than I need.
>
> I do not know why I do it—the houses are only a burden. But I have done it, and all my friends who have acquired wealth have big houses. Even so unostentatious a man as Henry Ford has a much bigger house at Dearborn than he really cares about.
>
> I wonder why it is. Perhaps it is some foolish survival of the ancient feudal idea when a big house meant a strong house in which one might keep a small army for protection. In a few cases, a big house is built just as an advertisement that one is rich; sometimes a big house is built so that great entertainments may be given.
>
> But in most cases, and especially with men who have earned their own money, the house is

just built, and when it is done, no one quite knows why it was ever started.

The houses are only a burden . . . I do not know why I do it . . . I wonder why it is. I admire his honesty, but the admission is astounding.

Reggie Vanderbilt's grandson—broadcast journalist Anderson Cooper—was one of the first Vanderbilt heirs who was never promised dynastic wealth.

It may have been a blessing. He's not only the most successful Vanderbilt heir in over a hundred years, but appears to be the happiest.

Cooper once said of inheritance: "I think it's an initiative-sucker. I think it's a curse. From the time I was growing up, if I felt like there was some pot of gold waiting for me, I don't know if I would have been so motivated."

Free from the inherited obsession with money, he was allowed to find his passion and appreciate the value of a dollar. It's like he was the first in his family to cut the strings of the marionette doll, refusing to let money control who he was or the life he lived.

Back to the difference between rich and wealthy.

What I find fascinating are stories like the Vanderbilts'. They were the richest people on earth but, by my definition, some of the least wealthy. Money to them was less of an asset and more of a social and mental liability, indebting them to a status-chasing life that left most of them seemingly miserable.

No matter how much money you make, anyone can get caught in that trap. And my gosh, I hope you avoid it.

If you want an example of someone I'd call wealthy, have a look at Chuck Feeney.

Feeney, who cofounded Duty Free stores, died in 2023.

The well-known part of Feeney's story is that he was the most frugal billionaire to ever live.

He gave away 99.99 percent of his $8 billion fortune years before he died. He and his wife kept $2 million, lived in a small apartment, flew coach, and lived a quiet life.

The less well-known part of Feeney's story is that he once gave the high life an honest try. *The Washington Post* wrote of his life in the 1980s, when he was newly rich:

> He had luxury apartments in New York, London and Paris and posh getaways in Aspen and the French Riviera. He hobnobbed with the other mega-rich on yachts and private jets. If he wanted it, he could afford it.

He quickly realized it wasn't for him. Society told him he should want those things. But it wasn't what actually made him happy.

Giving money away was.

"I'm happy when what I'm doing is helping people and unhappy when what I'm doing isn't helping people," Feeney said.

I love that.

Or more specifically: I love that he loved that.

He didn't follow a typical path of what other people told him to like or how to live.

He didn't worship his money and let it dictate how he should live, or control who he was, or capture him to a status-chasing life.

He found what made him happy, and used his (enormous) wealth as a tool to become even happier. He may have looked frugal, but he was actually the freest, most independent person you'll ever hear of.

He was *wealthy*.

Feeney is someone I consider a role model, not because of how much he made or the lifestyle he lived, but because he was so clearly in control of the money he had, never letting it become the master of his life. If the Vanderbilts were a family built "upon no better basis than the possession of money," Feeney was the opposite. He was a man built upon morals and individuality who just happened to have a ton of money. Rather than a monument to be glorified, the money he had was a tool that was used no differently than how a mechanic uses a wrench.

Everyone, at every income level, can learn from that.

My friend David Perell once wrote:

> The people I admire most have a way of escaping the bubble of culture. Sometimes via religion; sometimes via old books; sometimes via time in nature. Without such an escape, propaganda

wins. You stop thinking for yourself. Modern delusions grow into an all-consuming mind virus.

That's such a big part of the rich-versus-wealthy idea. To be happy, you have to be yourself. If you blindly accept money's ability to persuade your personality and dictate how you spend your day, it will quickly take control.

When putting this theory to use in my own (non-trust-funder, non-billionaire-tycoon) life, I keep three things in mind.

There's this idea in relationships that you can't be happy with a partner if you can't be happy without them. It's the same for spending money.

Recall the fascinating finding from behavioral finance that having more money is more likely to make you happy if you were already happy before you had more money. And the flip side: Beyond a basic level of necessities, it's hard for more money to make you happy if you're not already happy with who you are.

Your morals, your values, your personality, your friendships, who you seek attention and admiration from—you must control these things regardless of how much money you have in order to have a decent life. The danger is assuming that more money will improve them; that's when the money you have—or even just your ambitions for more—take control over your life.

If you're already satisfied with who you are, you naturally

view money as a tool to be used to make things even better. That's when you become wealthy.

Separate what you like from what you want.

They can be very different things. Many people like cigarettes because they feel good, but few actually *want* them. I like aimlessly scrolling through social media, but I don't necessarily want to do it—these things are just addictive, and they control the person rather than becoming tools to help to enhance the person's life.

What I want to buy are things that I both like and don't drive me crazy when I can't have them all the time—an occasional fancy meal, an annual big family vacation, nice clothes every once in a while. If for whatever reason I had to drop these things from my spending, it might sting a little, but my family and I would be fine. I enjoy these things, but I don't obsess over them—they don't control me. I think then, and only then, do you know that money is being used as a tool to help you rather than a master to obey.

There's a Stoic saying—"You are unlikely to have a good and meaningful life unless you can overcome your insatiability"—that fits well here.

Don't be proud of your consumption. Be proud of what you've built.

The family you've built, the friends you've found, the memories you have, the wisdom you've accumulated. There are times when the stuff you buy can help produce memories and foster quality time with friends and family. But the people, not the stuff, are what are actually meaningful.

Warren Buffett once noted that he has very rich friends who have everything—the big homes, the private planes, even hospital wings named after them. "But the truth is that nobody in the world loves them," he said. "If you get to my age in life and nobody thinks well of you, I don't care how big your bank account is, your life is a disaster."

You've become rich, but wealth remains elusive.

UTILITY VS. STATUS

The value of anything is its ability to help you live the life you want. Nothing more.

I once heard someone say that a high-end Toyota is a nicer car than an entry-level BMW, because the Toyota is filled with things that make driving more pleasant—plush seats, a great sound system, a moonroof—while the low-end BMW is mostly just bragging rights.

I love that framing.

The nice Toyota decked out with all the options has *utility*. It makes your life better. You're owning it for yourself.

The low-end BMW has *status*. It (might) change other people's opinion of you. You're owning it for them, and their attention.

It's such an important distinction to make when spending money. Maybe the single most important one, because it gets right to the point of whether you're using money as a tool to live a better life or as a yardstick to measure yourself against others.

An imperfect model I use in my own life is thinking like this: If my family and I were stranded on an island with no one else around to notice us, and we could have any material goods we desired, what would we own?

In this situation you would instantly value utility over status. You'd value comfort over appearance, the right fabric

more than the right logo, function more than brand, dura-
bility more than prestige, practicality more than size, a great
view over a prestigious zip code, and social interaction more
than social hierarchy. You'd want a high-end Toyota, not an
entry-level BMW. You'd want utility over status.

I'm not against buying things just for status. Fitting into
your chosen social group is an important part of a happy
life, and the social benefits of high status can be enormous
for those who pull it off.

What I find fascinating are cases when people confuse
the two. And it's so common.

People sometimes think they're buying something nice
because it will make their life more pleasant, comfortable,
interesting, or fulfilling. But unknowingly what they're paying for is a chance that other people will look at them, ide-
ally in a positive light.

With everything you purchase it's vital to identify which
is which—why you actually want to buy this thing—and realize that each offers a very different outcome and benefit.

Billionaire Bill Koch said one of his brothers collects money,
another collects women. He prefers wine.

Koch's cellar once contained a world-class collection of
over forty-three thousand bottles. He loved it. "You can taste
the love of the vintner," he says, calling drinking rare wine
"drinking history" that amounts to a religious experience.

Some of Koch's bottles were the finest and rarest ever

sold: He once paid $400,000 for four bottles of wine al-
legedly owned by former President Thomas Jefferson. The
bottles have Jefferson's hand signature scrawled right on
them. When Koch heard they were for sale, he said, "I gotta
have that." And that was that.

It was an amazing treasure he enjoyed showing off—
until historians from Jefferson's estate told Koch the bottles
were entirely fake.

Thus began a research project to authenticate Koch's wine
collection. He hired private investigators who discovered—
which perhaps will not surprise you—that several hundred of his most expensive and coveted wines were cheap
fakes.

Counterfeit wine is a massive business. Same with counterfeit handbags, sunglasses, shoes, and jewelry. The National
Crime Prevention Council says $2 trillion of counterfeit goods
are sold worldwide each year—the largest illicit trade in the
world.

A big part of the reason counterfeits have proliferated in
recent years is because scammers have become so good at
making authentic knockoffs that even experts struggle to
identify.

It's such a curious thing when you think about it.

Some goods are expensive because they are deemed to
be of superior quality. But even astute buyers, and the premium brands themselves, often struggle to spot counterfeits because the quality of the fake product is often . . .
pretty comparable to the real thing.

One of the scammers who took Bill Koch was an Indonesian wine enthusiast named Rudy Kurniawan. He was arrested in 2012 for running a massive fake-wine operation. Kurniawan got away with selling fake wines to some of the most astute wine drinkers in the world for years because his fake wine didn't just look good—it *tasted* so good, so authentic. He was a master at blending together cheap wine, slapping on a fake label that made collectors salivate, and selling for absurd prices.

The same thing happens with fake handbags. In 2016 a woman was sentenced to prison for buying $400,000 worth of handbags from department stores, returning identical counterfeit handbags to those stores, and reselling the real ones online. She got away with it for years because the fake purses she returned to the stores were so convincingly authentic.

If the taste of a fake wine or the quality of a fake handbag is indistinguishable from the real thing, you should not be bothered if your goal is utility. But so often it is not.

What you wanted was status.

You wanted to show others, and know for yourself, that you own something few others can have. It makes you feel better about who you are and what you've accomplished.

Which, again, no problem with that! Of course I do it sometimes myself.

But buying a thing for its utility versus its status offers a totally different experience and outcome.

Author David Brooks once wrote about a trip to Africa. He and his family stayed in seven different locations—some modern and luxurious, others camp-style with no running water. After the trip Brooks and his family realized they enjoyed the lower-end homely camps more than the nice hotels. At the cheap camps they got to socialize with locals and meet other guests. His kids played soccer with the staff. At the expensive hotels they were isolated in cocoons of sterile safety. That was the entire allure of the nice hotels—"stay here and you will hardly notice any difference between Midtown Manhattan and the Serengeti." But it wasn't at all what his family actually wanted. The pursuit of luxury and perhaps status detracted from the utility of the trip.

Utility being hijacked by the pursuit of status is so common in everyday life. Think about the burden of maintaining a house that's bigger than you need, or the stress you feel from buying a nice car you can barely afford. Status devouring utility is one of the most common frustrations of modern spending.

"People are often bad at knowing how to spend their money," Brooks wrote. "When we get some extra income, we spend it on privacy, space and refinement . . . but suddenly we look around and we're on the wrong side" of the line separating what makes you happy from what makes people look at you.

Thinking status is worthless isn't the point. That can actually be disastrous—if you don't care what anyone thinks of you, there's a decent chance that *no one* thinks about you. You'll find yourself cut off from the social world that can be the most important element of happiness in your life.

But you might find valuing utility more than status important for two big reasons:

Buying things for their utility gives you the ability to express your own identity, while chasing status often makes you conform to others' identity.

Almost by definition, the pursuit of status is the pursuit of showing other people what *they* want to see. That can be dangerous in a world where people are so different— different in tastes, different in goals, different in skills. You can find yourself spending so much time and money putting on a performance for people you don't even like, because they're so different than you are, especially when you're honest about who you are and what you want out of life. Conforming to others' views is a sacrifice that has a real, but hidden, cost in life.

Utility, by contrast, is deeply selfish in a beautiful way. Your top goal becomes bettering your own life and those you care about, the opinions and attention of others be damned.

As a writer, I've always believed in what I call "selfish writing." I write for an audience of one—*me*. I write stories I find interesting about topics I find useful, without wondering if readers feel the same. Not only is it more enjoyable, but I think it produces better work: The common writing phrase "know your audience" can quickly turn into "shamelessly pander to your audience" in a way that ruins a lot of writing.

The same idea can apply to so much in life, including how you spend money.

When you value utility over status, what actually happens is that you value individuality over conformity. The result, just like in writing, can not only be more fulfilling, but produces a better result. By letting yourself be yourself, without pandering to what others might want you to be, you get to focus on what you're good at and what actually makes you happy.

Give it a shot, and you'll probably find that you're extremely talented at being yourself, but a poor actor of what you assume other people want you to be.

The pleasure you get from utility can be more durable than pleasure gained from status.

The key to success in so many areas of life is endurance and longevity. I'm not interested in anything that's unsustainable.

Spending money on status can be rewarding, but it's often short-lived. Even when you're successful at gaining others' attention, you often just immediately shift your gaze to the next notch higher on the social hierarchy in a way that leaves you no more fulfilled than you were before. Status is fickle, and the trends society measures you by change every few years, forcing you to adapt whatever the cost. It's not a cheap game.

The brain is also very good at answering whatever questions you throw at it, and constantly flooding your mind with thoughts about whether you are impressing other people is a fast track to feeling inadequate and insecure.

Utility spending tends to be more durable.

I have no idea what kinds of things will impress other people ten years from now, but I know with near certainty that I will value comfort, dependability, convenience, and—most importantly—spending quality time with people I love and admire.

I wrote in my book *Same as Ever* that "things that never change are important because you can put so much confidence into knowing how they'll shape the future," allowing you to invest heavily in them. I know that when I'm ninety years old I will value a home with a nice view and memories with my kids—so I can invest in the utility those things provide. But certain clothes, jewelry, a big home, a fast car . . . what looks awesome today can look ridiculous—even embarrassing—a mere year from now, as you and society change. It's such a simple idea that can profoundly shift how you think about spending money.

Next, a haunting story about an actor's last words.

RISK AND REGRET

Good advice is never as simple as saying "Live for today"
or "Save for the future." The only good advice is
"Minimize future regret."

ctor David Cassidy's last words were "So much wasted
time."

What a terrible thing to realize when it's too late.
And I wonder if it'll become more common as many of us
spend our days aimlessly scrolling our social media.

Daniel Kahneman once said an important part of becoming good with money was having a well-calibrated sense
of your future regret. You need to accurately understand how
you'll feel about your current decisions at various points in
the future.

I love that observation; it's so powerful.

Maybe *regret* is the best definition of risk. When dealing
with money, risk isn't how much you might lose. It's not even
necessarily how you'll feel when you lose it—over time, a lot of
painful experiences turn into cherished lessons. Real risk is the
regret (or lack thereof) that might come years or decades later.

That concept plays such a big role when thinking about
how to spend money.

One of the biggest conflicts when managing money is
finding the delicate balance between the two most powerful
forces in the world:

- **Compound interest**, which turns patience today into fortunes tomorrow.
- **The fact that you are one day closer to death than you were yesterday,** so make the most of your short time here and enjoy every day you're lucky enough to be alive. There is a Scottish proverb: "Be happy while you are living, for you are a long time dead."

The struggle is knowing how much you should invest for the future versus spend today.

It's not an easy problem to solve. And it's a deeply personal one—not the kind of thing you can fit in a one-size-fits-all formula.

Let me tell you a story about animals' lifespans to drive home what I mean.

Spare a thought for the poor guppy fish, who lives a miserable existence but teaches us something important about anticipating the future.

Small, brightly colored, and terrible at defense, the guppy faces an unusually high rate of predator attacks. Birds eat guppies. Small fish eat guppies. Big fish eat guppies. Crabs eat guppies. It's everyone's favorite lunch.

How does a species under so much threat avoid extinction?

In short, guppies get busy as soon as they're born. They can reproduce at seven weeks old, and deliver new offspring every thirty days. By the time a six-month-old guppy is eaten by a bird, it might be a great-great-grandmother. The family lives on.

But this evolutionary trick has a nasty flip side.

Knowing how much danger they're in, guppies expend nearly all their energy on reproducing from the moment they're born. They grow as fast as possible, then devote a huge portion of their resources to nourishing their young. That leaves little energy left to care for themselves. Their bodies are thrown together slipshod, like cheap plastic toys, and few resources are available for cell repair and maintenance. By the age of a year or two, the guppy is a crusty senior citizen, crippled by disease and decline, soon to go belly-up.

That's how it should be: there's no use investing in the future when you're likely to be eaten anyway. It's the ultimate YOLO—"you only live once"—life philosophy.

Now compare the guppy with the Greenland shark, whose life is nearly the opposite.

The Greenland shark has no natural predator. It rules its habitat like a dictator.

With few threats, it takes its sweet time becoming an adult. It's one of the slowest-growing creatures we've discovered, reaching sexual maturity at—and this isn't a typo— 150 years old.

In the meantime, it spends more than a century devoting its energy to building itself a perfect body. Slow and methodical, with all of its resources going to cell repair and maintenance, it becomes virtually immune to cancer and infectious disease.

It's the ultimate long-term investor, saving for its future, devoting today's resources to ensuring it can have a good life literally centuries from now. As best we can tell, a Greenland shark can live for five hundred years, maybe more.

The point is that nature is extremely good at assessing future risk and allocating resources accordingly.

For guppies, nature takes a realistic look at future threats and says, "There are so many risks lurking. Don't even bother trying to plan for the future." For Greenland sharks, it says, "Your future is clear and foreseeable—plan away with confidence."

Most animals are masters at this balance, allocating resources between "invest for the future" and "live for today" as efficiently as possible.

But people trying to forecast the trajectory of their life?

Or how much they should spend today versus save for tomorrow?

Or how long they might actually live?

Or what they'll regret?

They tend to be terrible at it. What biology has mastered, modern human emotions have failed at.

To paraphrase Nassim Taleb, the world is split evenly between those who don't know how to start spending money and those who don't know when to stop.

You see this in popular financial philosophies.

On one end of the spectrum you have the FIRE (financial independence, retire early) movement, which promotes extreme savings and an almost pathological devotion to frugality. It sounds prudent, but it can be incredibly dangerous. In his book, *Die with Zero*, Bill Perkins writes:

Imagine if, by the time you died, you had done everything you were told to do: you worked hard, saved your money, and looked forward to financial freedom when you retired. The only thing you wasted along the way was . . . *your life.*

On the other end of the spectrum is the YOLO crowd, which pumps day-trading bankrupt penny stocks and crypto memecoins to become rich as soon as possible, with a sneering disdain for those investing for long-term stock market appreciation. A twenty-two-year-old who used his day-trading profits to buy a yellow Lamborghini is their unofficial hero. You know exactly how that story eventually ends.

The financial philosophies that are most appealing often risk the most amount of future regret. Author Nick Maggiulli says: "Taking too little risk is like smoking cigarettes, taking too much risk is like doing heroin. Both will harm you, the only difference is how quickly."

And the richer society becomes, the harder this problem gets.

For most of history the majority of Americans were the economic equivalent of guppies, living in such a precarious financial state that the mere thought of saving for retirement—or literally the *entire concept* of retirement—was out of the question.

As we became wealthier, we're now lucky enough to have to answer questions about how to save for a future while enjoying today that would have seemed preposterous to previous generations.

One hundred years ago, a twenty-two-year-old could expect to live until age sixty-two. Today, a twenty-two-year-old is asked to start saving for a retirement that might begin at age sixty-two and last another three decades—one third of young women in America can now expect to live to age ninety. One kid from every kindergarten class today can expect to live past age one hundred, an entire generation after they might expect to stop working.

At the same time, that twenty-two-year-old worker likely earns substantially more than their grandparents did at the same age, and has access to more opportunities to spend money that didn't exist a generation ago. They have more opportunities to spend on travel, concerts, dining, and same-day-delivered stuff that their ancestors couldn't conceive of. We're so fortunate to live in a world with so much opportunity to use money *right now* to experience a good life.

Those two things—saving for tomorrow while still living for today—cause so many people so much angst. The irony is that the richer society becomes, and the longer we live, the more opportunities we have to screw up our finances in a way that could leave us with regret.

I'm not immune.

I've been a big saver and long-term investor for my entire adult life. I love the idea of compounding and delayed gratification.

But I don't want to suffer the same fate as David Cassidy, looking back at the end of my life and realizing that I squandered my short time on this earth, denying myself an enjoyable life out of slavish devotion to building wealth.

I've also noticed an important shift in my thinking, one that might apply to many of you.

It's grim to think about, but no information in the world would be more powerful than knowing exactly how much time you have left to live. It's so powerful that a lot of people say they wouldn't want to know even if they could. It would be too scary, and would take the mystery out of life.

But almost nothing in your life would be the same if you knew.

I met someone a few years ago. When we parted ways he said, "Life is long. I hope we stay in touch."

Life is long. No one says that. They always say, "Life is short." But obviously it could be either. We have no idea.

The "life is short" philosophy says don't wait, go have fun, live a great life—eat, drink, and be merry for tomorrow we die. If your life were shorter than you expected, nearly everyone would follow that advice. You'd also be likely to forgive, forget, and not be bothered by petty annoyances, realizing that with your limited time to enjoy good stuff there's no use being bitter. You'd appreciate every sunset, smell the flowers, and call an old friend. You wouldn't miss a single one of your kids' Little League games. Part of the reason former President Lyndon Johnson had so much energy and ambition is because he always feared he'd die young.

What about the "life is long" philosophy? If you knew you'd live to be 102 years old, you probably wouldn't feel as rushed today. You'd be less anxious about your career. You wouldn't feel guilty sleeping in, taking a sabbatical, or using all of your vacation pay. You'd plant trees to watch them grow and take more pictures to remember. You'd be more willing to learn a new skill. You'd take better care of your joints, and long-term investing would be more exciting.

But the truth is no one has any idea how long they'll be around. I find it useful, though, to think about what it would be like to realize you're near the end at different points in your life.

The idea of being on my deathbed looking back with regret at a life of missed opportunities—the vacations I could have taken, the cars I could have purchased—changed as soon as I became a father.

I have young kids. When I do the grim mental exercise of imagining being at the end of life tomorrow, I think I'd be relieved and proud to realize that the material sacrifices I made to save more money will provide my wife and kids with a meaningful nest egg.

The alternative—being about to die and realizing that your young family is about to face a financial burden because you spent so much—would leave me wracked with guilt. *So much regret.* That, to me, would cause me to look back at all the trips and dinners and spending and think, "So much wasted time." Time I could have used to provide a better future for my family.

But will I still believe that in thirty years, when hopefully my kids are settled and independent? Probably not. At that point I'd mostly regret the trips I didn't take, the experiences I didn't go for—the memories I didn't make.

I don't think those are contradictory feelings. And I'm OK if you disagree; all behavior makes sense with enough information. But I think they highlight an important truth that applies to everyone:

Good advice is never as simple as saying "Live for today" or "Save for the future." The only good advice is "Minimize future regret."

That's it. I think that's the best we can do when trying to find the balance between living for today and saving for tomorrow. Attempt to minimize your regrets with an understanding that different people will regret different things, and you yourself will regret different things as you age.

Amazon founder Jeff Bezos once described his decision to start an online bookstore in the 1990s:

> The framework I found which made the decision incredibly easy was what I called the regret minimization framework.
>
> I wanted to project myself forward to age 80 and look back on my life and I want to have minimized the number of regrets I have.
>
> And I knew that when I was 80 I was not going to regret having tried this. I was not going to regret trying to participate in this thing

called the internet that I thought was going to
be a really big deal.

But I knew the one thing I might regret is
not ever having tried.

And I knew that that would haunt me every
day. So when I thought about it that way it was
an incredibly easy decision.

Two things stick out to me here. One is how sound this
advice is. The other is that the specific example wouldn't
apply to me and my personality (I likely would regret devoting that much time and energy to something that failed).
Everyone's different, which is why the blanket advice of "live
for today" or "invest for tomorrow" can miss so much real-
world nuance. The only good advice is to minimize your future regrets.

Since everyone's different, I can't tell you how to do that.
But here are two ideas I think about with my own financial
decisions.

1.   Good memories are the closest thing to living for today
while compounding for tomorrow.

The anonymous Twitter account FedSpeak once wrote, "The
purpose of life is to experience things for which you will
later experience nostalgia."

I can't be alone in realizing that as I get older, memories

of things that took place ten, twenty, thirty years ago are some of my most cherished assets. They aren't financial assets but, boy, they are very real assets nonetheless.

The amazing thing about memories is how they can compound over time, just like a stock. When I was ten years old, memories of what I did at age nine were boring. Today, those same memories are astounding and hilarious to recall as I can put them into the greater context of my life. In fifty years, they will be my most cherished possessions.

I once heard an elderly woman say that the benefit to growing old was the ability to time travel in your head—to remember what life was like in, say, the 1950s and compare it to today. Or to ponder in amazement at how much technology has improved since you were a kid. Children are rich in health but poor in life memories; as you age, that flips.

Typical advice that is nearly cliche at this point is to spend money on experiences, not things. It's not bad advice. But the way it's framed leads people to think the only way to do that is to spend money on a nice vacation or to travel to some distant land. That's not always the case. I can think of many expensive experiences that would be entirely unmemorable, while memories formed with friends during high school might be some of your fondest, and likely cost nothing.

I try to keep in mind that the things I am most likely to regret in the future will be the time I didn't spend with my kids, the relationships with friends I didn't put enough effort into, and certain things I'm stressed and anxious about today that I'll eventually realize deserved more self-forgiveness.

It might not cost any money to nurture those things. But

there are cases where money can help, just not in the way you think.

Spending money on a vacation with my kids could form valuable memories. Having a career that pays less but lets me spend more quality time with my kids every day might lead to much happier memories.

It can be hard to contextualize, but say you can choose between one job that pays $60,000 per year and requires forty-five hours of work per week, or another that pays $50,000 per year and requires thirty-five hours per week. The latter "costs" you $10,000 per year in lost income, which over thirty years invested at 8 percent is something like $1 million. But it gives you back five hundred hours per year, which, over your career is fifteen thousand hours of potential memories doing something you enjoy. And those memories compound over time just like assets.

People love to gawk at the power of compounding when investing their money. It's much harder to think about the value of compounding memories you get by trading money for time, but the results can be just as incredible.

It could easily be the best money you ever "spend," and the ultimate antidote to regret.

2. Saving for the future creates independence today.

If I save $100 for the future, what does that cost me *today?*

I don't think the answer is $100, or anything close to it.

Sure, I could have used that money today to buy a $100 shirt or a $100 dinner with friends.

But by saving it for the future, I gain something today: *$100 in independence.*

One hundred dollars in options and freedom to do anything I want in the future that costs $100.

One hundred dollars of time that I might need at some point.

One hundred dollars of reduced stress about my ability to care for my family or retire when I need to.

That can be as tangible a benefit to me *today* as buying the $100 shirt.

Once you view savings as providing the benefit of independence, you stop viewing saving for tomorrow as sacrificing today.

I will tell you personally: The degree of financial independence I have that's come from saving my entire life is among my most valuable, useful, and enjoyable assets *today*. I don't feel like I'm just saving for the future. Savings has given me independence that allows me a degree of doing what I want, when I want, with whom I want, that makes today—right now—better than it would have been if I had saved less in the past.

Of course it's a balance—everything worthwhile in life is. Independence is the most enjoyable when you also have the ability, financially and psychologically, to spend what's necessary today to create memories with the people you want to. But it's too easy and too common to assume that saving for the future prevents enjoying today, when in fact the two go hand in hand, joining forces in a way that guards against regret.

Now for a story about how disastrous envy can be.

COPYCATS

A parable: A teacher stands before her class and says, "Here's a math problem. There are ten sheep on a farm. One sheep runs away. How many sheep are left?"

A student raises his hand and says, "Zero. There are no sheep left."

"It appears you don't understand math," the teacher says.

"No, it appears you don't understand sheep," replies the boy.

The urge to watch other people and copy what they're doing without asking questions is so powerful, so pervasive, and explains so much of modern life.

Let's dig deeper.

LOOK AT THEM

*Jealousy, envy, and the priceless art of not caring
what others think.*

B uzz Aldrin became one of the most famous humans
on the planet on July 20, 1969, when he walked on the
moon.

It was an astounding feat, possibly the most incredible
thing humans have ever accomplished.

But Buzz was the second human to walk on the moon,
stepping foot on the lunar surface minutes after Neil Armstrong. Fellow astronaut Michael Collins once explained of
Aldrin, known to be cantankerous and for fame not wearing
well on him: "I think [Buzz] resents not being first on the
moon more than he appreciates being second."

Jealousy is such a powerful thing. It's difficult to appreciate what you have and what you've accomplished, because
beyond a basic level of necessities, what you often want is to
place yourself in a higher ring of the social hierarchy. So
everything you've accomplished is relative to other people,
and you often crave most whatever someone else has but you
don't.

That's important for spending money, because for so
many people the question of whether you're buying nice
things is actually "Are these things nicer than other people's

things?" The question of whether your home is big enough is actually "Is my home bigger than my neighbor's?"

It's understandable and unavoidable. A lot of life is a competition for resources—for money, time, mates, attention, friends, land—where what matters is not how good you are, but how good you are relative to other people. Russian biologist Georgii Gause became famous for an ecology concept now known as Gause's principle, which says that two species competing for the same limited resources cannot coexist—one will always outcompete the other until it's extinct. So of course it's natural to constantly look around at others, mildly paranoid, driven by what they have and you don't.

But let me make a point that's critical but easy to overlook in the art of spending money: There's a fine line between being *motivated* by what others have and you don't (potentially good) and being *envious* of what they have and you want (always dangerous).

Being motivated by what others have can be fun—their success is like an effective form of advertising for things you didn't know existed. But being envious of others is mental torture, like a contract you've made with yourself to be miserable.

Few topics are as important because we all look around at others, potentially jealous of what they have, and set our spending desires accordingly.

When entrepreneur Josh Kushner was in college, a wealthy friend took him to a Knicks basketball game. The seats,

Kushner recalled, were astounding—courtside, like you could literally smell the players. He was in awe. Then Kushner's friend looked five seats over and said, "My seats are good, but that guy's seats are better."

The author C. S. Lewis once defined this feeling so well in an essay called "The Inner Ring." Life, he described, is often viewed as a series of social rings, and people's desire is to break into the next level, the more exclusive ring. If you're outside of a ring, nothing seems better than the thought of being on the inside. But once you're on the inside of one ring, you realize you're not nearly as happy as you thought you'd be, and you shift your attention to the next ring, where nirvana seems to reside.

So much of life is like that: a constant struggle of viewing other people as having something we want, and then once you have that thing, you spot yet another person who has something new that you want, and around and around you go, ever disappointed.

Lewis wrote: "Unless you take measures to prevent it, this desire is going to be one of the chief motives of your life, from the first day on which you enter your profession until the day when you are too old to care."

And he wrote that more than eighty years ago! It's so much worse today. J. P. Morgan's observation that watching your neighbor become rich undermines your financial judgment was true when he said it more than a century ago—today, *everyone* is effectively your neighbor, where social media turns envy and comparison into an Olympic sport.

When it comes to envy, jealousy, and spending money, let me share a few of the most important points to keep in mind.

- It's nearly impossible to "win" the status game. What's unique and enviable in one period becomes common and bland in the next.

Wired magazine's founding executive editor Kevin Kelly once told me something I loved: If you want to know what lower-income groups will aspire to spend their money on in the future, look at what higher-income groups exclusively do today.

European vacations were once the exclusive playground of the rich. Then they trickled down.

Same with college. It was once reserved for the highest-income groups. Then it spread.

Same with investing. In 1929—the peak of the Roaring '20s bubble—5 percent of Americans owned stocks, virtually all of them the very wealthy. Today, 58 percent of households own stocks in some form.

Same with two-car households, lawns, walk-in closets, granite countertops, six-burner stoves, jet travel, and even the entire concept of retirement.

Part of the reason these products spread to the masses is that they got cheaper. But the reason they got cheaper is because there was so much demand from the masses—hungered by their aspirations—that pushed companies to innovate new ways of mass production. And it shows why you can't permanently win the status game: What makes something high status is the fact that others don't have it. Once they eventually get their hands on that thing, it's no longer high status.

Author Rob Henderson once noted that when he was a student at Yale, his classmates loved the Broadway play *Hamilton*. But once the play was released on Disney's streaming platform—available to the masses—they hated it, found it boring, and stopped talking about it. The Yale students didn't care about the play as much as they cared that they could watch something others couldn't. *Hamilton* was cool when it was exclusive to their social ring; much less so when anyone could watch it.

People like to mimic those who appear to be living better lives, which can make those in enviable positions always feel uneasy and never satisfied, because they are constantly being chased by others who covet their lifestyle and possessions. That's why you can never truly win the status game—it's a moving target.

When you realize that status is a game that is never permanently won, you see why chasing it can be so unfulfilling.

- **Being jealous of what others have and assuming your life would be better if you were like them is misleading because you are not getting a full picture of their lives.**

If I want what you have, I overlook that you want what someone else has and therefore you feel exactly like I do. And that someone else wants something another person has, on and on, like one continuous chain of social envy.

Once you realize how never-ending the status and jealousy game can be, you realize the only way to win is to stop playing.

- **Being jealous of what others have is outsourcing your critical thinking to strangers.**

As natural as social comparison is, it's a depressing thing to ponder when you think about it. If you left me alone with my friends and family—people I love and whose attention I really want—I would form one set of desires. But when you expose me to a group of millions of strangers who I don't know and don't care about, I form a completely new and grander set of desires.

One of my favorite writers, Lawrence Yeo, once wrote:

> Envy is inversely correlated with self-examination. The less you know yourself, the more you look to others to get an idea of your worth. But the more you delve into who you are, the less you seek from others, and the dissolution of envy begins.

That's so smart. If you view one of the main goals of money as being independent, you start to view social comparison as its nemesis.

I want to fit into the social group I choose, and spending money to look a certain way or occupy my time a certain way can be part of that. But once you anchor your expectations to an endless group of strangers, you are assuring yourself that you'll never be independent, or even satisfied.

Here's an easy way to show what I mean: Telling someone they are jealous is always an extreme insult, because no one wants to admit that they are chasing what others have. They want to think they're independent, because—deep down—independence is the goal. Envy is admitting to inferiority.

The more you know yourself and become closer to what you want, the less you envy others even when they have what you don't.

- **FOMO—the fear of missing out—is one of the most dangerous financial reactions that exists.**

FOMO is the intersection of social comparison and recklessness. You see someone with something you want and lose all inhibition to get it.

Having no FOMO might be the most important financial skill. Being immune to the siren song of other people's success—especially when that success is sudden, extreme, and caused by factors outside their control—is so powerful and important that it's practically impossible to do well over time without it. When strategizing, Dwight Eisenhower used to quote Napoleon, who said a military genius is "the man who can do the average thing when everyone else around him is losing his mind." It's the same with money.

FOMO is recklessness masked as ambition. You see someone else getting rich or living a great life and think, "If they can do it, I can too." That feels like a good emotion—it feels like you're learning through observation and following a data-driven path to success.

But what's actually occurring is you are outsourcing your emotions to people whose quick windfall or flashy life has probably left them in a fragile emotional state to begin with. If you chase them, you might follow them right over the cliff. An astounding example of this in play: A study by three researchers once showed that if your neighbor wins the lottery, you are more likely to borrow money and go bankrupt in the future.

Charlie Munger once said: "Someone will always be getting richer faster than you. This is not a tragedy. . . . The idea of caring that someone is making money faster than you are is one of the deadly sins."

Remove FOMO from the equation and what's left?

You only care about your own financial goals.

You only care about the opinions of those you care about.

You think long term and avoid getting sucked into fads and bubbles.

And you don't need much else to do well over time.

- **Your propensity to be jealous of what others have can increase as you become wealthier.**

If you can't afford rent or food, the desire for more money is existential, and has a very clear objective and finish line.

But if you're already financially comfortable, the desire for more money is mostly about status, which has no upper limit and is insatiable.

Researcher Suniya Luthar once did a study of teenage mental health, drug, and behavioral issues among poor inner-city kids. As a control group, she compared them to rich suburban kids—who, in a shock to many, were comparatively much worse off by several metrics. One theory is that when rich kids are surrounded by other rich kids, the urge to climb the insatiable social ladder explodes. Free from the burdens of struggling to pay rent and buy groceries, your entire life becomes a quest to become richer and more popular than the person next to you.

I've seen this so often. When you have everything you need, you immediately shift to focusing on everything you might want, which is a never-ending list. When you're poor, you want a stable paycheck and a small house. When you're rich, you want to be on the *Forbes* list of billionaires and have a private jet—the curve of social comparison grows exponentially with income.

It sounds crazy, but sometimes I think the most status-starved and money-hungry people are rich celebrities because their social comparison group are ultra-rich mega-celebrities.

Realizing that your aspirations—and for some people, their entire sense of self-worth—can anchor to the social group you closest associate with makes you think harder about who you choose to associate with. Which brings me to the most important point:

• **Be careful who you socialize with.**

Good advice for a lot of things in life is to remember that you are a reflection of the three or four people you socialize with the most.

If your friends have expensive tastes, your expectations converge on that lifestyle. If your friends' idea of an awesome Friday night is skipping rocks into a lake while chatting about life, your material expectations stay more grounded.

Everything worthwhile in life is just the gap between expectations and reality, and when your frame of reference is rich people trying to impress each other, that gap can close quickly.

I used to live in the woods in the middle of nowhere, then I moved to the beach in Los Angeles. It was stunning how quickly my definitions of *success, rich,* and *luxury* exploded once I became surrounded by rich people. Ambition can be a wonderful thing, but I'm not sure it is a positive thing overall: A dentist or small business owner can feel like they're swimming in wealth and success in one town but like an improvised failure by comparison to peers in another.

Who you socialize with can have as big an impact on your material happiness as how much money you make and how much you spend. When you think of it that way, you choose wisely who you spend your time with.

———————

C. S. Lewis ended his essay by noting, "The quest of the Inner Ring will break your hearts unless you break it."

What breaking it meant was simple: Once you become satisfied with whatever ring you currently reside in—jealous of no one, envious of nothing, appreciative of what you have and what you're good at, grateful for friends and family—you "are indeed snug and safe at the center of something which, seen from without, would look exactly like an Inner Ring."

A lack of envy brings another gift: freedom. Let's tackle that.

THE SIMPLEST FORMULA FOR A PRETTY NICE LIFE

How to live a good life is endlessly complicated, but sometimes the best way to understand a complicated topic is to pay close attention to the few big rules that carry the most weight.

Let me propose one: The simplest formula for a pretty nice life is independence plus purpose.

Independence plus purpose.

Independence plus purpose.

Independence plus purpose.

The independence to do what you want, and the wisdom to want to do meaningful things.

It's not everything, but, boy, does it move the needle.

There are many ways to be independent—being free from poor health, cultural influences, and an arbitrary boss. But financial independence is obviously a big one.

Spending on independence can be the most wonderful thing money can buy. And it's more in your control than you might think.

That's the next chapter.

WEALTH WITHOUT INDEPENDENCE IS A UNIQUE FORM OF POVERTY

Money you haven't spent buys something intangible but valuable: freedom, independence, and being able to spend time in your own way.

The people I look up to the most are not necessarily the richest or most successful. Almost always, they're the freest. The most in control of their own lives.

It took me a while to realize that. "Rich" to me used to mean having lots of fancy toys. Now it means not being hurried, spending time with my family, control over my schedule, and intellectual independence. Doing life my way.

Independence. That's true rich.

A related perspective I hold—one that many either disagree with or find counterintuitive—is that there's no such thing as unspent money. You spend every single cent you've ever earned. You spend every dollar in your bank account, whether you know it or not.

Money you haven't spent buys something intangible but valuable: freedom, independence, and being able to spend time in your own way. Every dollar of savings buys a claim check on the future. (And every dollar of debt you hold is a piece of your future that someone else controls.)

I've always been a big saver. But I've never viewed my savings as idle money. I've never even viewed it as saving up for a purchase in the future.

I view every cent of savings as a ticket toward a greater degree of financial independence, which is my true goal.

If I move $500 into my savings account, I view that as having purchased $500 of independence. It has almost no different meaning to me than if I had purchased a $500 television—the money is "spent" in either scenario, just spent on different things that offer different value.

And I spend *frivolously* on independence.

I blow tons of money on having control over my calendar.

I have no budget for how much I'm willing to spend on autonomy and spending time with the people I want, when I want to, for as long as I want to.

For me, independence has the highest ROI, more than anything else I've spent money on.

That whole idea—trading money for time, rather than trading it for stuff, because having more time is going to provide greater joy in your life—is probably the most overlooked aspect of spending money, because to most people the extra time and mental clarity you get from independence and savings doesn't feel like "spent" money.

Let me tell you a quick story about two athletes, each of whom made lots of money, but used it in different ways.

Antoine Walker made $108 million playing twelve seasons in the NBA. Call it $25,000 a day.

After Walker signed a six-year contract in 1999, Boston Celtics president and coach Rick Pitino said Walker "will never have to worry about money again in his life."

Walker agreed. "I thought I was set for the rest of my life," he said in 2015—which was five years after he filed for bankruptcy.

During his playing years Walker had, by his own count, "six or seven cars" that were replaced when he saw someone driving a nicer one, a personal payroll that included supporting thirty friends and family, and a house for his mother that had ten bathrooms and a full-sized basketball court. He allegedly never wore the same suit twice. He gambled millions in casinos.

The final score before the bankruptcy judge was $12.7 million in liabilities against $4.3 million in assets. He's now a financial advisor to athletes, admirably begging players to learn from his mistakes.

John Urschel had nowhere near the same level of athletic talent or stardom.

A fifth-round pick of the Baltimore Ravens in 2014, Urschel played three seasons and made even fewer headlines as a player. He earned less in his entire career playing football than Walker did every eleven weeks playing basketball. His salary—about $600,000—was close to the league's minimum wage.

But the way Urschel chose to spend his earnings was astounding.

He lived a fine life, luxurious by any standard. But he saved the vast majority of his paycheck.

Why?

"I'm thankful for the money I was able to make," he said. "I'm not a billionaire, but I'm at a point where I'm financially stable. I don't ever need to worry about money."

And by all accounts he did not.

He retired from football in 2017 and went back to school to get his PhD. He's now a professor at MIT.

But the point is he could have done whatever he wanted.

The takeaway is not "Live less like Walker and more like Urschel." They're the extreme ends of the spectrum.

But let me ask: Whose life—not their sports talents, but the life they lived—do you admire more?

This is not a trick question.

I'm willing to bet you admire Urschel more than Walker. Even if Walker didn't go bankrupt but merely stretched himself thin and had to give up some of his luxuries, you'd probably still admire Urschel's outcome more. Most people would.

That's because Walker lost control of his life. He reached a point where his decisions—where to live, what to drive, even what clothes to wear—were dictated by a bankruptcy judge.

But Urschel maintained control over his life. He could do what he wanted, when he wanted. His life was his own canvas to paint.

And that—control over what you're doing—is actually what people admire. They admire it because it's what they actually want. They want it because it's what makes people happy.

Nassim Taleb says, "What matters isn't what a person has or doesn't have; it is what he or she is afraid of losing. The more you have to lose, the more fragile you are."

So many people—regardless of income—have a lot to lose because they are so reliant on other people for their security and satisfaction.

As I'm writing this, I read this morning in the newspaper a story of a CEO who was once worth several hundred million dollars whose bankers are liquidating his assets, because he borrowed so much money that he now can't repay. Bankers sold his yacht and his home. The debacle got him ousted from his company.

I was struck: Here's someone in the top 0.001 percent of income and wealth with less financial independence than someone you might consider to be poor.

Wealth without independence is a unique form of poverty.

———

It's easy to scoff at the mere mention of financial independence, because it seems like something reserved for spoiled trust-funders and billionaires. I once had a friend who refused to save any money because it all felt so trivial to him. His view was: Why save $50 when it moves the needle by so little?

That's a mindset that I'd like to break.

Financial independence is not black or white. It exists on a spectrum. At every point on the spectrum—every additional dollar of savings—you move up a little bit, and your life can improve a little more.

Here's how I view the spectrum of financial dependence and independence. Do yourself a favor and find yourself on this list:

Level 0: Total financial dependence on the kindness of strangers who have no vested interest in your success. Think of panhandlers and CEOs asking for government bailouts. You have a complete lack of control over the direction of your financial life in a way that leaves you vulnerable to a fragile, often cruel world.

Level 1: Complete financial dependence on people who want you to succeed because they like you and their reputation is attached to your success. Think about kids under age fifteen who are supported by their parents but too young to work. Borrowing money from friends and family who realistically know you can't repay them also fits this category.

Level 2: The ability to partially support yourself by adding value for others while still somewhat reliant on external support. Young people who work but still rely on their parents to support what they consider basic lifestyle necessities fit this category. Same for workers who rely on government assistance and semi-retired workers who rely on pensions. A major part of your financial well-being relies on the decisions of people who may or may not keep it going in the future.

Level 3: The ability to fully support yourself by adding value for others, but with a value that is marginal and easy to replace. This is a common category for both people and businesses. It is grinding and tenuous. It smells like independence in the sense that you can pay all your bills, but a boss or customer still owns your day and can dictate your future. Your future relies on their decisions. If you lose your job, you may struggle to find a new one, and you have little savings to fall back onto.

Level 4: Enough savings to cover run-of-the-mill problems. You can endure hassles that every person should expect to experience on a regular basis without getting wiped out. A small medical bill, you're OK. It's cold and you need to spend more on heating this month, you're OK. Your kid needs new pants, you're OK. This is the level at which you realize that having literally just a few dollars in savings provides a small degree of independence over life's hassles.

Level 5: Enough savings to cover larger, unforeseen problems. You still rely on the whims of your boss to get by month to month, but if a crisis struck, you'd probably be OK for a reasonable period of time. Your car breaks down, you're OK. Your furnace breaks, you're OK. You now have some degree of independence and protection against what you might consider "bad luck" in life's day-to-day risks.

Level 6: Some retirement savings, education savings, and the avoidance of credit card debt. You feel like you have one hand on the financial independence wheel. You still rely on bosses, but you can foresee a time down the road when your current savings will grow into a new level of independence for you and your family. You may not be fully independent, but you have sufficient hope that both fuels your optimism and helps you sleep at night.

Level 7: The ability to pick a job that avoids the most egregious examples of bullshit and unnecessary hassles in your life. You still rely on a boss for your paycheck, but have the freedom and marketable job skills to say, "No, not you. You're a terrible boss. And this is a terrible job. I'll find someone else to work for." A big part of this is having sufficient savings that allows you to both quit when you want to and take the time you need to find a new, better job. (This is a wonderful and realistic goal for the majority of people. If you make it to level 7, you're crushing it.)

Level 8: Becoming comfortable enough with your socioeconomic status that you don't feel the need to show off to strangers. This is the first glimpse of not just financial independence, but intellectual and identity independence. The inability to do this is a hidden form of debt and dependence.

Level 9: The ability to avoid most debt, including auto loans, student loans, and even mortgages. Debt can be cheap capital, but it keeps you beholden to strangers who own a piece of your future decisions. I once knew a guy who hated his job and had a clear vision for what he would rather do, but felt like he had to stay at his job to be able to repay his student debt. The debt, therefore, cost so much more than its interest rate: It cost him his career independence. A similar fate hits people who borrow so much for their house that they're stuck in a city they no longer want to live in if they can't sell their home for more than they borrowed. Once you view debt as a claim check on your future options, you stop asking, "What is the interest rate?" and start wondering, "How much independence is this going to cost me?"

Level 10: Few realistic economic situations would cause you or your family to be pushed back below Level 5. You could support yourself for a year or more off your liquid savings if you got hit by a medical emergency or a huge recession. It's the first true stage of financial independence. You can now say "No, go away" to almost anyone, or any employer—or any economic event—with high odds of recovering from the repercussions.

Level 11: Passive income like interest and dividends covers a meaningful portion of your living expenses. You still work for a paycheck, but your portfolio is now providing enough income to reduce the common stresses and time commitments that restrict most people's independence. It's common for this level of independence to be owed to a slim lifestyle as much as a large investment portfolio. Once you taste this independence, you realize that lifestyle desires can compound faster than almost any asset.

Level 12: Your investments and their reasonable return expectations will cover basic living expenses for longer than your life expectancy. Congrats—you are no longer reliant on others for work. You can deal with them if you want, and you probably will. But only if you want, when you want, with whom you want, which feels amazing. Many people reach this level with self-funded retirement savings.

Level 13: Your assets and their reasonable return expectations cover above-basic living expenses. You can live the lifestyle you prefer and have something left

over for family or charity. "Above-basic" expenses can be defined however you want. It varies by person. Just be careful about unnecessary lifestyle creep that can pull this independence down like gravity, and remember what comedian Chris Rock says: "If Bill Gates woke up with Oprah's money he'd jump out the window."

Level 14: Your independence lets you do and say what you please, unconcerned with other people disagreeing with you, since you don't rely on the financial support or opportunities they could offer you. One note here: The concept of f**k-you money—having so much money that you can tell people to f**k off without fear of repercussion—is great. But so is kindness and civility.

So I aspire to "no thank you, I'm not interested in that, I respectfully disagree and I'm free to ignore you" money. One is rationalizing being a jerk, the other is intellectual independence.

Level 15: You wake up every morning realizing that you can spend your time doing what you want, with whom you want, for as long as you want. Bosses don't control your day. Social debt doesn't influence your decisions. Actual debt doesn't control your options. You beat the game. And you realize that while this doesn't guarantee happiness and there are still plenty of opportunities for you to screw up your life, you have unlocked a lifestyle boost that 99.99 percent of humans who have ever lived have not experienced. The only risk is that you forget how grateful you should be to be in this situation.

Regardless of where you sit on this spectrum, and regardless of how high you aspire to get, the key is realizing that independence is a spectrum.

Independence is not something you either have or don't have—it's not binary like that.

Every little bit of savings, and every little bit of lower expense, pushes you higher on the independence spectrum.

Now, some people value independence more than others. Some people want to be higher on the spectrum than others. There's no right answer on how much you should want.

But too many people don't bother chasing independence because it seems out of reach, when in fact they could easily—at any income level—be improving their independence spectrum, and in turn improve their lives.

The trick is viewing every bit of savings as having actively purchased something, even if it doesn't come with a receipt: You have purchased the ability to do what you want, when you want, with whom you want, for as long as you want. And it is priceless.

HUSH MONEY

I think bragging is the inverse of how satisfied you are with life. It's one of the most reliable psychological formulas around.

In the movie *Broadcast News,* Tom Grunick asks, "What do you do when your real life exceeds your dreams?"

Aaron Altman replies: "Keep it to yourself."

The more you want people's attention, and the more you try to focus that attention on how smart, rich, and successful you are, the higher the odds that you're trying to fill some sort of emotional hole.

When I see people clearly bragging about how much money they make or spend, I try not to judge. I'd rather ask: Who are you trying to impress, what do they actually think of your boasts, and is your bragging unintentionally doing more harm than good?

SOCIAL DEBT

*When how you spend your money influences what
people think of you in unwanted ways.*

F rank Lucas was a drug dealer, and a very good one at
that. By the 1970s his heroin empire in New York City
was bringing in $1 million per day. Day after day, year
after year.

Part of the reason he got away with his crimes for so long
was that he kept a low profile, living a mostly unremarkable
material life, which helped him avoid unwanted attention.
He wasn't on the police's radar.

But hubris caught up, as it has a way of doing.

Other low-level drug dealers lived flashy lives, and eventually Lucas had had enough. He wrote in his memoir: "I
could not have people who made less money than me walking around thinking they ruled the world. I screamed it out
to all who would listen: 'Ya'll think you gone outshine me?'"

At the March 8, 1971, "Fight of the Century" between
Muhammad Ali and Joe Frazier at Madison Square Garden,
Lucas wore a floor-length $100,000 chinchilla coat with
matching hat—clothes worth roughly $1 million in today's
dollars. He sat in the best seat, in front of Frank Sinatra and
Vice President Spiro Agnew.

"For the first time ever, I actually felt like showing off,"
he wrote.

It worked. Strangers lined up to take pictures with him and his fancy coat. The press went wild. Everybody that night paid attention to Frank Lucas.

Including the New York Police Department.

"I came to the fight an unknown man," Lucas wrote. "I left that fight a marked man."

Stunned at how an unknown man could be living like a king, law enforcement began investigating Lucas, and that was that. He was caught, arrested, and sentenced to seventy years in prison.

Lucas was a criminal. But let me introduce you to a concept that applies to all of us ordinary people. I call it social debt.

Social debt is what happens when how you spend your money influences what people think of you in unwanted ways. It's often a hidden form of debt, which makes it especially dangerous.

Sometimes it's people being envious of you.

Sometimes it's you suddenly feeling superior to people whose company you used to enjoy.

It can even be your own higher expectations that come from inflating your lifestyle.

There are some purchases for which every dollar you spend changes how the rest of the world thinks of you, and what you think of yourself, in ways you might come to regret.

––––––––––––

An important topic in pharmacology is called the Arndt–Schulz rule, which states that "for every substance, small doses stimulate, moderate doses inhibit, large doses kill." A little bit of sun exposure is healthy, even necessary. A moderate amount can cause sunburn. Way too much can cause lethal cancer. Same for alcohol, tobacco, caffeine, and even mental anxiety. There's a tipping point when helpful stimulation turns to danger, then disaster. And it's often very difficult to know the tipping point until it's too late.

Money works in the same way.

It sounds crazy, but I think there's an "ideal" net worth for everyone, when money not only stops bringing pleasure but becomes a social liability.

Your ideal net worth threshold might be different from other people's. But for most people, the level is lower than you probably imagine, because the more money you make and spend, the more social debt seeps into your life.

A few years ago I read a story about lottery winners who lost everything. A common denominator of these stories is that lottery winners often quickly become overwhelmed—even bankrupt—by social debt. The minute people learn how much money they have, friends, family, and strangers feel entitled to ask, beg, and steal in a way that leaves the winners not only broke but socially exploited.

Take the tale of one of the winners:

> After winning $3.9 million in October 1985 and $1.4 million four months later, Ms. Adams found that she no longer had the privilege of privacy. "I was known," she said, "and I couldn't go anywhere without being recognized."

A problem that's easy to overlook with money is that assets are simple to measure but liabilities can be hidden. Measuring how much you won in the lottery is simple: $3.9 million, down to the penny. But how do you measure losing your privacy? Or the nagging doubt that some friends only like you for your money? That's way harder. Tiger Woods is a billionaire. That asset is easy to measure. But he once admitted that he loved scuba diving because it was the only place in the world where no one recognized him and no one asked anything of him. How do you measure that depressing social liability? It's not on any spreadsheet, but it's a very real debt in his life.

Henry David Thoreau once explained this concept well. How much an item costs is so much more than what you see on the price tag. "The cost of a thing is the amount of what I will call life which is required to be exchanged for it, immediately or in the long run," he wrote.

I once spoke to a group of NBA rookies. We discussed how to avoid the common tragedy of athletes who make a fortune in their twenties and are bankrupt by age thirty.

One player mentioned something I found so insightful. He said most people think athletes go broke because they frivolously blow their money on jewelry and cars. Sometimes that's true, but the most common cause of athletes going broke is social debt.

"When you grow up in poverty and then you're making $10 million when you're twenty-two, that's not your money," he said. "That's Mom's money, Dad's money, Grandma's money, cousins' money, friends' money. You can't just tell them 'I got mine, good luck to you all.'"

Athletes buying themselves a mansion wasn't the problem; it was buying a modest house for their fifth cousin whom they'd never met but felt obligated to help that pushed athletes to bankruptcy.

These might seem like rich-people problems. But social debt creeps up everywhere, in its own way, for normal people.

The more your identity becomes attached to your physical possessions, the more other people's thoughts about you influence your spending decisions, and the more eager you are to constantly wow those people with something newer, bigger, better, and more expensive. So the cost of the new car that you think will impress people is not, say, $50,000—it's $50,000 *plus* the $60,000 car you'll feel pressured to replace it with in two years just to keep the spotlight on you. There's an ironic saying, "It's very expensive to be rich," which is as true as it is absurd. The expense comes when people desperately try to keep up with spiraling social debt that's attached to living a rich lifestyle.

Another way social debt creeps into your life is your own expectations. I used to ride the Amtrak train from DC to New York City regularly. The train has a "quiet car"—a section where everyone is supposed to be quiet so you can sleep or get some work done. People use the quiet car because they want serenity, but it was astounding how often it backfired. When you expect quiet, you become ultra-sensitive to the slightest noise. If someone in the quiet car speaks in more than a whisper, the entire car plunges into a state of deep irritation. I'd bet that sitting in the "peaceful" quiet car actually leaves people with higher blood pressure.

The same thing happens when you buy nice stuff.

Maybe you didn't mind when your old car was dirty or dinged—but now that you bought a nicer car, you can't stand it when it gets muddy, and you lose your mind when someone scratches it in the parking lot. That angst is a social debt, and some people who own nice things are nearly bankrupt with it.

Maybe when you bought a new, bigger house, you thought you'd be happier. But then you realize that the reason you wanted a nicer house was to socially compete with other people who had nice houses. So once you got a nice house, you just started dreaming about even nicer homes. Once you accept that having the nicest home in your social group is your goal, it becomes not only an obsession but a game that cannot be won, since the group you compare yourself to shifts with each new, nicer house that you buy.

The more money people have, and the more they spend, the more social debt they tend to be burdened with. Past a certain level of basic spending, every notch of higher lifestyle comes with social obligations, judgments by others, and shifts in your own expectations that are very real liabilities but easy to ignore.

The point is not to say you should avoid nice cars and nice homes—I like both. It's a realization that once money goes from being a tool you can use to make yourself happy to a symbol of what other people measure you by, you've lost the game. Author Kent Nerburn once wrote to his sons:

> I want you to know that possessions are chameleons that change from fantasies into responsi-

bilities once you hold them in your hands and
that they take your eye from the heavens and
rivet it squarely on the earth.

I once did some consulting for a family that was worth
$8 billion. If you googled their name, nothing came up.
No *Forbes* list, no gala photos, no profiles, no Wikipedia
pages . . . nothing.

That was intentional.

They mastered what so many other people—the rich, the
middle class, the aspiring rich, and everyone in between—
failed to recognize. They lived the most amazing life you
could imagine, *and* they had virtually no social debt.

They had total freedom, privacy, and independence. They
chose their friends carefully and gave money away anony-
mously. Their lack of social debt may have been their most
valuable asset.

It reminded me of what Naval Ravikant once said: The
best position to be in is rich *and anonymous.*

It's a wonderful sentiment, but still leaves us with the
question: How do ordinary people like you and I avoid social
debt? How do we actually become rich and anonymous, so
our spending decisions don't influence our social lives in
disastrous ways?

My strategy is called quiet compounding. That's the next
chapter.

QUIET COMPOUNDING

The fastest way to get rich is to go slow.

N ature is not in a hurry, yet everything is accomplished," said Chinese philosopher Lao Tzu.

Giant sequoias, advanced organisms, towering mountains—nature builds the most jaw-dropping features of the universe. And it does so silently, where growth is almost never visible right now but staggering over long periods of time.

It's quiet compounding, and it's a wonder to see.

I love the idea of quietly compounding your money. It's perhaps my most cherished and important financial belief, because it's so simple but encapsulates so many powerful financial traits we've already discussed in this book. And just like in nature, it's where you'll find the most impressive results.

Every few years there's a story of a country bumpkin who has no education and a low-wage job but manages to save and compound tens of millions of dollars.

It's the same story over and over: They just quietly saved and invested for decades. They never bragged, never flaunted, never compared themselves to others or worried whether their investments trailed their benchmark last year. Their entire financial universe—their thoughts, their goals, their beliefs—was contained to the walls of their home, which allowed them to play their own game and be guided by nothing other than their own desires. That was their superpower. It was actually their only financial skill, but it's the most powerful one of all.

They were masters at quiet compounding.

Regardless of the lifestyle you live or how much money you spend, it is such a powerful idea to grasp.

Imagine if, after your first date with a partner, you had to make every phone call, every text, every conversation with that person public on social media. Or even just with a small group of friends and family. You know what would happen: People would tell you you're doing this wrong, you're doing that too much, you should say more of this and less of that, on and on. You'd be so embarrassed, nervous, and influenced by other people's goals and different personalities that *you wouldn't be you*. No relationships would work.

Money is similar. People become so nervous about what other people think of their lifestyle and investing decisions that they end up doing two things: Performing for others, and copying a strategy that might work for someone else but isn't right for them.

Let me reiterate the two ways to use money: One is as a tool to live a better life. The other is as a yardstick of success to measure yourself against other people. The first is quiet and personal, the second is loud and performative. It's so obvious which leads to a happier life.

Quiet compounding means a few things to me:

1. An emphasis on internal versus external benchmarks.

I've found it helpful to always ask, "Would I be happy with this result if no one other than me and my family could see it, and I didn't compare the result to the appearance of other people's success?"

Remember that it's impossible to win the social-comparison game because there's always someone getting richer faster than you. Once you stop playing the game, your attention instantly shifts internally, to what makes you and your family happy and fulfilled. It makes it so much easier to enjoy your money, regardless of how you choose to spend it.

2. An acceptance of how different people are, and a realization that what works for me might not work for you and vice versa.

Christopher Morley said, "There is only one success—to be able to spend your life in your own way."

So many financial mistakes come from trying to copy people who are different from you.

So be careful who you seek advice from, be careful who you admire, and even be careful who you socialize with. When you do things quietly you're less susceptible to people with different goals and personalities telling you you're doing it wrong.

My friend Brent Beshore says, "I am 100% happy to watch

you get really rich doing something that I have no interest in doing." You can apply that philosophy to how people spend and save their money too. We're all different. Life isn't zero-sum. Live and let live.

3. A focus on personal independence over social dunking.

Once you do things quietly you become selfish in the best way—using money to benefit your life more than you try to influence other people's perception of your life. I'd rather wake up and be able to do anything I want, with whom I want, for as long as I want, than try to impress you with nice stuff.

4. A realization that quick wealth is fragile wealth.

Money that was earned quickly tends to be loud, while quiet compounding is a long-term endeavor.

That's important, because how quickly your money was made can greatly influence how you manage it. I love the idea that the speed in which you made your wealth is the half-life for how fast you can lose it. Double your money in a year? Don't be surprised when you lose half of it just as quickly. It's the same in business: Blitz-scaling? Blitz-failing.

Two things happen with quick, fragile wealth.

One is that money that comes easily tends to be spent easily. When money comes quickly, the emotional cost of blowing it on something frivolous is low. You are only careful with something when it's dear to you. Spending quick money that you didn't invest much time or energy into earning can feel like the equivalent of a one-night stand: impulsive and prone to regret. That's why old money wants a tax shelter and new money wants a Lambo.

The other is that the quicker the wealth was made, the higher the odds it came from luck that will revert just as fast. If you experience a quick windfall and ratchet up your lifestyle accordingly, the pain you'll feel when the windfall can't be repeated can be existential.

When you accept these realities, the beauty of quiet compounding—slow, inconspicuous, nonperformative, on your own terms—becomes so clear.

5. An appreciation that the fastest way to get rich is to go slow.

What happens when quiet compounding becomes your goal? The first thing is that you feel less pressure to perform for others. And when you stop performing for others, your attention naturally peers further out into the future, as you ask how to create a better life instead of seeking more attention.

That allows you to foster one of the most powerful financial skills: endurance.

A great irony in finance is that the fastest way to get rich is often to go slow. You're never in a rush, never impatient, rarely worried or influenced by others doing things differently. You know that longevity and the ability to keep something going for the longest period of time is the true magic of finance. Like so many things in life, speed gets all the attention but slow has all the power.

A lot of people want to be long-term investors but struggle to actually do it. One reason is they get caught up in comparison—comparison to peers, benchmarks, and wondering what other people will think of them if they find out they lost money in the last six months.

In investing, long-term money success is about being able to absorb manageable volatility; if you can't do that, you're pushed into the much harder trick of attempting to avoid short-term volatility. You're only durable when you care more about surviving volatility than looking dumb for getting hit by it in the first place.

Instead of trying to look smarter than everyone else, you make a quiet long-term bet that things will slowly get better over time.

You're not in a hurry, yet everything is accomplished.

Now for a discussion about what happens when you look in the mirror and all you see is money.

IDENTITY

When money controls who you are.

M oney is like gasoline during a road trip," says author Tim O'Reilly. "You don't want to run out of gas on your trip, but you're not doing a tour of gas stations."

One of the most common ways that money stops being a tool, and becomes a master, is when your financial goals and beliefs become part of your identity.

Everyone's different, but my identity is: dad, husband, son, friend. That's what's truly important to me and what I base my life around. If I can use money to enhance those things, great. But never do I want money to *be* one of those things.

Harvey Firestone, then one of the richest men in America, wrote in his 1926 biography about how he often missed the simple life he lived before he became wealthy:

> I paid twenty-five dollars a month for a little house—our grocery bill hardly averaged five dollars a week. Sometimes it seems that it might be better to go back to those simpler days, that one might get more out of a less complex life. . . . But it cannot be done. . . . One changes with prosperity. We all think we should like to lead the simple life, and then we find

that we have picked up a thousand little habits which we are quite unconscious of because they are a part of our very being. There is no going back—except as a broken man.

He wanted to go back to his simple life, *but there was no going back except as a broken man because being a rich man became part of his very being.*

What an admission. And what an example of what happens when your relationship with money becomes an ingrained part of your identity.

Investor Paul Graham has a saying: Keep your identity small.

"The more labels you have for yourself, the dumber they make you," he writes. "If people can't think clearly about anything that has become part of their identity, then all other things being equal, the best plan is to let as few things into your identity as possible."

Anytime in life you say, "I am a . . ."—regardless of what it is—you've formed an identity. And identities are so important that people will often go to absurd lengths to defend them.

Let me share the most common financial identity that can harm people in ways they never imagined.

"I am a saver."

It seems like such a good trait, and it sounds so innocent. And of course both are true. But a lot of financial planners will tell you that one of their biggest challenges is getting clients to spend money in retirement. Even an appropriate, conservative amount of money. Frugality and saving become such a big part of some people's identity that they can't ever switch gears.

I call it frugality inertia. It's what happens when a lifetime of good saving habits can't be transitioned to a reasonable spending phase.

I think what many people really want from money is the ability to stop thinking about money. To save enough money that they can stop thinking about it and focus on other stuff.

But that ultimate goal can break down when your relationship with saving money becomes an ingrained part of your personality. You struggle to break away from focusing on money because the focus itself is a big part of your identity. You associate life success with your bank account going up, up, up, and you're never able to actually spend it, even in a reasonable way.

If you develop an early system of saving and living well below your means—congratulations, that's great. But if you can never break away from that system, and insist on a heavy saving regimen well into your retirement years . . . what is that? Is it still winning? Those whose ultimate goal is to stop thinking about money are stuck. Refusing to recognize that you've met your goal can be as bad as never meeting the goal to begin with.

Charles Darwin once noticed that some animals have traits that hinder their survival—peacock feathers that attract predators, or huge antlers that hinder maneuverability when being chased. Why didn't evolution find a fix? It was

simple, Darwin reasoned: Some traits are beneficial for reproductive success even if they pose a long-term risk. There are
so many examples of this in nature, with evidence that a
particular gene related to reproductive success in humans is
also linked to Alzheimer's disease. Nature is very good at
promoting one behavior even if it comes with some harm
down the road.

It's so similar with money. Once you get ingrained with
one smart behavior—a good saving regimen, or a way of
spending money that you enjoy, or even an investing
strategy—you run the risk of becoming blind to when it
might be reasonable to do something different, and you've
set yourself up for eventual trouble. Anytime you've formed
a money identity—I am a saver, I am a rich person, I am a
poor person, I always buy this, I always buy that—you've
formed a roadblock to eventually switching gears, changing
your mind, or trying something new.

It's common in investing, where people take on labels
like "value investor," "trader," and "tech investor." The labels
seem harmless, but once you label yourself you've formed
an identity that can prevent you from seeing the big picture,
finding other opportunities, or changing your mind when
you need to.

At some level these labels can turn cult-like—the FIRE
movement (financial independence, retire early) in particular started with a worthy goal (financial independence), but
that goal can become so ingrained in its followers' identities
that they quit jobs they may have enjoyed, harming their social lives and leading to boredom.

Who is in control at that point—you, or your devotion to a financial philosophy?

I once met a guy whose parents are multibillionaires, and have been for decades. This guy—now in his forties—grew up in a life almost none of us could imagine. Multiple mansions. Private jets. Chauffeurs. Butlers. Everything money could buy, as much as he wanted, whenever he wanted it.

And I was astounded to quickly learn when I met him that he was so regular. So down-to-earth, so humble, so polite, so empathetic, genuine, and—dare I say—relatable. Whatever the opposite of spoiled is, he seemed to be it—which is astounding given the life he was raised in.

I asked how his parents managed to pull that trick off. How do you raise a kid to be so normal when their surroundings are so extreme?

"It's not complicated," he told me. "Money has never been part of our identity."

What was, I asked?

"Loving each other, being good employers, being good citizens. That's what we talked about. And that's what we judged others by."

He said despite knowing from a young age that his family had more money and toys than anyone else he knew, his parents never so much as implied that this made them superior to anyone else. Money was a tool to leverage who they were, but it never controlled or defined who they were.

"When kids are spoiled and bratty, it's usually not just because their parents buy them a lot of stuff," he said. "It's because the parents teach the kids that having more than other people makes you better than them." And the parents of spoiled kids often come to believe that because making money, having money, and spending money is an integral part of who they are. They look in the mirror and that's what they see: money, money, money. "I am a person with money." That's their identity.

Even Charlie Munger—one of the most astute and rational financial minds of the last century—seemed to fall for being trapped by a financial identity.

Shortly before he died in 2023, the legendary multibillionaire Munger told an interviewer that "I could've done a lot better if I had been a little smarter, a little quicker."

"What are you talking about? You've had success in everything you've done in life," said the interviewer, CNBC's Becky Quick.

"Well, I might have had multiple trillions instead of multiple billions," said Munger.

"Do you sit around thinking about this? What would you have done differently?" asks Quick.

"Yes, I do think about it. I think about what I nearly missed by being just not quite smart enough or hardworking enough," says Munger.

You can interpret those comments many ways. He was a professional money manager, so having money tied to his identity was probably unavoidable.

But think about an ordinary person with the same

mentality—you've achieved financial success, you can retire, you can do what you want, but all you can think about is
how you could have made more money, saved more money,
invested more money. There are so many of these people.
Money is their identity.

And then you have to ask: Is the money serving you, or
are you serving it?

Is it your tool, or your master? Does it serve you, or do
you serve it?

A couple things to keep in mind to prevent your money from
infiltrating your identity in a harmful way:

***Value the ability to change your mind, change your lifestyle,
alter your spending, and try something new.***

The surest sign that something has become a dangerous
part of your identity, and controls you rather than the other
way around, is the inability to change your mind when you
or the facts change.

Visa founder Dee Hock had a great saying: "A belief is
not dangerous until it turns absolute."

Religion and politics are contentious because almost by
definition your beliefs are part of your identity—you're not
just dealing with ideas and philosophies, but tribes and be-
longing. Another Dee Hock quote also applies here: "We
are built with an almost infinite capacity to believe things

because the beliefs are advantageous for us to hold, rather than because they are even remotely related to the truth." Things get dangerous when people let their financial beliefs fall into the same category.

I love the concept of mental liquidity. It's the ability to quickly abandon previous beliefs and strategies when the world changes, you change, or when you come across new information.

So much of what people call "conviction" is actually a willful disregard for facts that might change their minds. It's dangerous because conviction feels like a good attribute, while its opposite—being wishy-washy—makes you feel and sound like you don't know what's going on.

The strategy of having strong beliefs, weakly held, is often helpful.

At my current age I strongly believe in saving for the future. But I'll be fine letting go of that strategy as I age, work less, and want to enjoy what I've saved. Same for what I like to spend money on today, and even the socioeconomic class I think I belong to.

The goal is to be able to live the life you want to live and have money serve you. You only get there when your financial beliefs aren't tied to your identity. Wanting more money than you need to be independent and happy is an accounting hobby.

Money should always be a tool to leverage who you are, not a goal in itself.

Recognize what true independent thinking looks like.

The best definition of independent thinking is when your beliefs on one topic can't be predicted from your beliefs on another topic. If you tell me what political party you belong to and I can instantly and accurately guess your views on immigration, abortion, taxes, and guns, are you really thinking independently, or just going along with your tribe?

It's the same with money. Particularly for those with an above-average income: If you tell me your salary, and I can accurately guess how much you spend on cars, homes, clothes, and vacations, are you using money as a tool to leverage your unique personality, or are you just going along with what society says you should want to spend your money on?

The people I know who've used money best have inconsistent spending habits. They spend a lot of money on this, and very little on that. They value this, and couldn't care less about that. They're independent thinkers, forcing their money to work for them, not the other way around.

It's like what poet Rudyard Kipling writes: "If you can talk with crowds and keep your virtue, or walk with Kings— nor lose the common touch," you're on your way to greatness.

Next, a discussion about what you need to keep identity from controlling your money beliefs: trying new things.

TRY SOMETHING NEW

I can't recommend this enough: Within the confines of your budget, experiment with as many types of spending as you can, cutting quickly and without mercy the things that aren't working for you.

F rancis Crick, who discovered the double-helix structure of DNA, was once asked what it takes to win the Nobel Prize. He responded: "Oh it's very simple. My secret had been I know what to ignore."

Lots of brilliant minds work like this. Albert Einstein once said that his main scientific talent was his ability to pore through thousands of papers and experiments, find the few that were important, and ignore everything else.

It sounds trivial: *Find what works and just do that.* Ignore the rest. Thanks, Einstein.

But there is so much wisdom in this strategy, and it applies perfectly to finding the thing you should be willing to spend money on.

First, let me tell you an idea I have about books.

When finding a new book to read, my strategy is to have a wide funnel and a strong filter. I want to start reading as many books as possible, but finish few of them.

Reading becomes a chore if you insist on finishing every book you begin, because the majority of books are either adequately summarized in the introduction or just not for you.

So insisting on finishing every book you begin can be a slog. It can be boring, unfulfilling, and a waste of time. And once you see reading through that lens, your willingness to pick up another book wanes. This, I've come to believe, is why some polls show that half of Americans don't read books at all.

Which, of course, is tragic. "The man who doesn't read good books has no advantage over the man who can't read them," said Mark Twain. Every smart person I know is a voracious reader who also says, "Every smart person I know is a voracious reader." There are so few exceptions to this rule.

There are more than four million books for sale in the English language. If you only pick up books that you know with certainty that you're going to enjoy—reading the same authors, the same genres, or the same topics—you are missing out on so many potentially life-changing books that you never realized you may have enjoyed.

The conflict between these two—most books don't need to be read to the end, but some books can surprisingly change your life—means you need two things to make the most of reading: lots of inputs and a strong filter.

You should be willing to start reading any book that looks even mildly interesting. *Anything.* Even the faintest tickle of interest should be enough to make the cut. Fiction, nonfiction, romance, military history, try all of it. You want the widest funnel possible, exploring as many new ideas as you can.

But then you need a strong filter. If the book isn't working for you, move on quickly.

The filter should be ruthless, taking no prisoners and offering no mercy. Similar to dating, a book you're not into after ten minutes of attention has little chance of a happy ending. You should feel no shame, no guilt, for failing to finish a book, even if you quit after the first few pages. There are so many good books out there. Go find a new one.

Since I started using this strategy, I have found so many amazing books that I never knew I would have enjoyed. I never liked fiction until I forced myself to try ten different fiction books, and found one that I loved. Same with history, which felt like the worst high school lecture until I finally found a few topics that I couldn't get enough of. Some books with bad reviews I loved. Other books with stellar reviews I couldn't make it past the first page.

What I learned: It's impossible to know what you're going to like until you try it, so you have to try everything. But the only way to try a million new things is to have a strong filter that immediately rejects what isn't for you.

And, boy, that is also so true for spending money.

There are so many different ways to spend money that are right for one person but crazy for another.

Some people live for international travel; others can't stand being away from home for any reason. For others it's nice restaurants; others don't get the hype and prefer cheap pizza. I know people who think spending money on first-class plane tickets is a borderline scam; others would not dare sit behind the fourth row. I have a friend who owns more than five hundred pairs of sneakers, which give him so much joy. I can't understand it for the life of me.

Author Ramit Sethi has advice that I love: You should spend extravagantly on the things you love as long as you mercilessly cut the things you don't. His specific example: He loves clothes, but isn't a car guy. So he dresses like a rich man and drives like money's tight.

If you disagree with Ramit's choices, you've discovered the point: Everyone's different. Everyone has their "thing." And the only way to find your thing is to try a million different things, rejecting what doesn't bring you joy until you find the odd thing that does. Spending money is an area of life where you want a wide funnel and tight filter.

I can't recommend this enough: Within the confines of your budget, experiment with as many types of spending as you can, cutting quickly and without mercy the things that aren't working for you.

Try spending more than you currently do on food, travel, clothes, sporting events, experiences, whatever it is. But immediately stop if it's not making you happier, just as if you were reading a bad book.

If you do this enough, you will find, by process of elimination, the potentially weird thing that's right for you to spend money on, and if you cut the other stuff that brings you no joy, you'll likely have enough money to actually spend on what makes you happy.

The more different kinds of spending you test out, the closer you'll likely get to a system that works for you. The trials don't have to be big: a $10 new food here, a $50 treat there, slightly nicer shoes, etc.

Albert Einstein and Francis Crick were not born knowing the fine details of their field—no one is. They had to sift through piles and piles of research, quickly rejecting what they found to be trivial. It's a useful strategy for spending money: There is no guide on what will make you happy— you have to try a million different things and figure out what fits your personality, ruthlessly cutting the rest.

Wide funnel, tight filter.

A few points are critical to understand in this endeavor to find your "thing":

If you can't find your "thing," there is a good chance that money has entrapped you, controlling your personality, and you are either addicted to saving money or ignorant of its potential, becoming unable to use it as a tool to provide joy in your life.

If you met someone who said, "I don't like food, any of it. I've never had a meal that I thoroughly enjoyed," you would immediately spot a person who hasn't tried enough food.

Money can be similar.

There's a line in the movie *Boiler Room* that goes, "People who say money can't buy happiness don't have any." I would amend that to say: People who say money doesn't buy happiness haven't yet found their thing. They should keep trying. Wider funnel.

And that doesn't have to be about material possessions. Your thing can be giving money away, or using it as a form of independence. Everyone has a thing if they just try hard enough to find it.

It's common for people to default to whatever society tells them they should like.

Which is usually that whatever product is most expensive will bring them the most joy.

Sometimes that's the case. Very often it's not even close.

Using price as a measure of how much joy you'll get out of a purchase can miss one of the most important lessons in business history: Premium prices are often found on branded products, and the purpose of a brand is not to signal quality. It's to signal consistency.

An important feature of life in the United States before 1850 is that most people never traveled more than a few dozen miles from their birthplace. Life was local. You ate food grown in your town. Your house was made of local lumber. Your clothes were sewn by a local seamstress. You knew the person who made them. That person was often yourself.

The industrial revolution and the Civil War changed that. Millions of people and soldiers were suddenly on the move, and railroads provided a way to transfer goods farther and faster than ever before.

Robert Gordon writes in his book *The Rise and Fall of*

American Growth: "As America steadily became more urban and as real incomes rose, the share of food and clothing produced at home declined sharply. . . . Many American men had their first experience of canned food as Union soldiers during the Civil War."

This was one of the biggest breakthroughs in history. But it posed a problem.

For the first time, consumers were disconnected from the person who made their food. For most of history, a bad product was either your own fault or could be taken up face-to-face with a local merchant. But canned food came from dozens of suppliers, none of whom customers knew or could identify. Without accountability, quality was horrendous. *Harper's Weekly* wrote in 1869: "The city people are in constant danger of buying unwholesome [canned meat]; the dealers are unscrupulous, and the public uneducated." No one knew who to trust.

The William Underwood Company solved this problem.

Underwood was one of dozens of canned meat suppliers. Recognizing that canned meat had a reputation for inconsistency, Underwood created a red devil logo consumers would recognize. It added a tagline: "Branded with the devil, but fit for gods."

The logo re-created the familiarity that face-to-face commerce had achieved for most of history. No matter what part of the country they were in, consumers who saw the devil logo knew they were getting a specific product made by a specific company under specific quality standards. They were happy to pay more for Underwood meat because it reduced the gamble they would otherwise take with an unknown product.

In 1867 Underwood took the logo to Washington, DC, and filed the first federal trademark. It was, in many ways, the nation's first brand.

The point is that brand has always been about signaling consistency. McDonald's does not make the best hamburgers, but you know that a McDonald's hamburger in Detroit will taste the same as one in Denmark.

There's value in that—and often a premium price to pay for it. But it means that so much premium pricing in a modern economy can be detached from the quality of the product. *You're not necessarily paying for quality, you're paying for consistency.*

When you realize that higher prices don't automatically signal higher quality, the need to experiment with more types of spending is even greater. I have found more joy out of a local hole-in-the-wall $7 burrito than I have at some famous five-star restaurants, and better T-shirts that cost $12 than others costing more than $100.

When you strip away the allure of a brand and focus on whatever makes you the happiest, a new world of opportunities arises if you're willing to experiment.

Learning what to quickly say no to can be more important than what to buy.

Trying a million new things doesn't work unless you foster the skill of quickly rejecting what isn't for you, like the bored reader who nods off after the first page.

Part of the danger with modern spending is the assumption that you're supposed to like what's advertised, popular, and expensive. Maybe you will. But perhaps you're falling hook, line, and sinker for the psychological power of advertising.

Knowing when to quickly reject the kind of spending that doesn't fit your personality is one of the most overlooked skills in money. It requires a fierce independence, free of being shamed into believing that what other people appear to enjoy is what's best for you.

I have a theory: The more susceptible you are to advertising, the less satisfied you are with your own life. You're desperate for someone to tell you what you should like because you haven't yet figured it out for yourself.

The solution is less about figuring out what to buy than it is rejecting what doesn't work for you—the opposite of falling for marketing.

Evolution, the strongest force in the world, teaches by destroying what doesn't work, selecting what does by process of elimination. Spending money can be the same. The wide funnel only works if you have a tight filter.

Nassim Taleb says, "You are rich if money you refuse tastes better than money you accept." As a corollary: You are spending wisely if the purchases you reject taste better than the ones you buy. The more you can say, "I tried buying this or that. It didn't work for me," the more you know you're on the right path.

Trying new things creates variety in life, which is a value all of its own.

There's a well-known idea that time feels like it speeds up as you age. Summer break feels like an eternity when you're nine years old but your sixties can skip by in a flash.

One theory for why this happens is that the perception of time relies on the number of new and surprising memories formed in a period. The monotony of commuting to work on the same road for twenty years passes without leaving a mark. But every day is a memorable surprise to a child experiencing her first summer camp, or learning how big the universe is for the first time.

Monotony makes time speed up, variety makes it slow.

So it is with spending money. New experiences and new products that you've never tried before add a level of excitement that's hard to replicate any other way. Even when the new purchase didn't work for you, the memory and knowledge you gain by trying something new can be more thrilling than the monotony of the same experiences repeated day after day, year after year.

Variety also protects you from the variability of life. Anthony De Mello, always wise, says, "If you learn to enjoy the scent of a thousand flowers you will not cling to one or suffer when you cannot get it."

Now let me tell you about money and kids.

WHAT MONEY CAN'T BUY

I once heard a story from a priest that I'll never forget.

This priest spent decades delivering last rites in hospitals. It's the kind of experience that puts you in a unique position: You become familiar with how people say goodbye to loved ones.

When a parent is dying, their children often go to the priest with a sense of despair. How do I say goodbye to a parent who was so instrumental in my life? How can I possibly tell them how much they meant to me?

The priest's advice to the kids is to go into the room, one by one, and thank the dying parent for the one thing they're most grateful for.

"In families that I know have had a lot of problems—strained relationships—the child will often thank the parent for something that cost money," he said. "Thank you for putting me through college. Thank you for putting food on the table. Thank you for buying me a car."

"In the best families, the ones I know have solid relationships," he said, "the kids say the same thing every time."

"Thank you for believing in me."

WHAT YOUR KIDS WANT

I once heard a story that went like this.

A dad played a game with his son every week. He offered the son a dime and a nickel, and told him to pick one.

The son picked the nickel every time.

His brother told him he's crazy, because the dime is worth more.

"No, because if I pick the dime, Dad might stop playing this game," the son replied.

If you're fortunate to have enough money to spend some on your kids—or your friends, your neighbor, your partner, whoever it might be—remember that the ones who love you almost certainly don't want your money as much as they want your love and attention.

YOUR MONEY AND YOUR KIDS

Values, hard work, support, and the opposite of spoiled.

John D. Rockefeller—then the richest man in the world—once walked into the Waldorf Astoria hotel in New York City. He needed a room while his home was being remodeled.

He asked the hotel agent for the cheapest room available. The agent said, "Mr. Rockefeller, surely we can get you something better. When your son stays here he takes the Presidential Suite."

Rockefeller responds, "Yes, but my son has something I've never had: a rich father."

Managing money and kids is so difficult. And this is not a topic that only applies to the very wealthy: Nearly 60 percent of American parents with kids aged eighteen to thirty-four have supported their kids financially in the last year. Middle-class families grapple with weekly allowances, how much financial support you'll offer your kids when they go off to college, and small inheritances.

But like so much with money, this is not a financial problem that can be solved on a spreadsheet. It's all psychology, sociology, and emotions. Money and kids might actually be the most emotional of all financial problems—I have yet to meet a parent who is totally unemotional about their children's financial future.

One of the most treacherous topics with kids and money is how you, as a parent, use your money to help them without spoiling them.

Charlie Munger was once asked by one of his rich friends if leaving his kids a bunch of money would ruin their drive and ambition.

"Of course it will," Charlie said. "But you still have to do it."

"Why?" the friend asked.

"Because if you don't give them the money they'll hate you," Charlie said.

Like a lot of Munger advice, I think this interaction is designed to be memorable.

But by and large, he's right. Those are the two options for the rich when giving money to their children: ruin their ambition with inheritance, or risk some form of strife by denying them an easy life.

Warren Buffett once said that he often hears rich people talk about how dangerous a welfare society is, creating a generation of moochers reliant on food stamps and unemployment benefits. But "these same people are leaving their kids a lifetime supply of food stamps and beyond," he said. "Instead of having a welfare officer, they have a trust fund officer. And instead of having food stamps, they have stocks and bonds that pay dividends."

Of course there are exceptions. But most of the exceptions—rich kids who inherit money without it impacting their ambition—are because the kids are special, not because the parents necessarily made a smart decision. If eighteen-year-old Bill Gates inherited $1 billion, it wouldn't have stopped his ambition. Same with Steve Jobs and Elon Musk. Mark Zuckerberg was offered $1 billion cash for Facebook when he was twenty-two and he didn't blink. Didn't even consider it.

But those are the rare birds. Most people need to be driven by fear of not making it.

My friend Chris Davis grew up in a wealthy household—his grandfather is legendary investor Shelby Davis, who turned $50,000 into almost $1 billion—and was told when he was young that he wouldn't see a penny because his family didn't want to rob him of the opportunity of making it on his own.

Chris now jokes: "They could have robbed me *just a little*."

It's never easy.

One nuance here is that it's dangerous for you, as a parent, to live one lifestyle while you demand your kids live a different, more modest one.

As a parent you may have good intentions for wanting to make your kids live a comparatively humble existence: to teach them virtue, hard work, and respect. But you risk teaching them something completely different, which is resentment.

To take an extreme example: If you fly first-class while making your kids fly in coach, the message you intend to send them is "Work as hard as I have and you may get this one day." But the message they may hear is "I am more worthy than you and enjoy watching you squirm."

Cornelius Vanderbilt once demanded that his son Billy quit smoking. "Your wish is sufficient," said Billy as he threw his cigar into the sea. Cornelius then reached into his pocket, pulled out a cigar, lit it, took a puff, and blew the smoke into Billy's face. You can laugh, but similar power moves occur when parents attempt to teach their kids hard work and frugality without practicing those values themselves.

A good friend tells the story that when he went on family ski trips as a kid, his grandfather would say, "If you want me to buy you a lift ticket, you first need to hike up the mountain once." The lesson the kids learned from the experience was not hard work and virtue. It was "Grandpa is an asshole." You can do as much damage trying to instill dignity in your children as you can by spoiling them rotten.

Every family finds their own way. But everything I've seen tells me that when kids are young and living with their parents, the parents and the kids have to live the same material lifestyle. So you, the parent, need to pick that lifestyle carefully. "You haven't earned what I have" can be a less effective message than "Let me teach you the value of hard work by doing it together." Lead by example, not by humiliation.

Another point here about picking your lifestyle carefully is the extent you, as a parent, set your children's lifestyle expectations when they're young.

If you're fortunate to have some disposable income and, say, buy a luxury car when you have young kids, but then your kids go on to decide to become kindergarten teachers and can only afford modest cars, do they feel ashamed? Like they failed relative to their parents? Will they in fact pick a career they don't enjoy but that pays well because they feel pressure to at least match the lifestyle they grew up with? Does my desire to give my kids a good material life today set them up for disappointment down the road if they can't afford the same lifestyle they grew up with?

Generational growth—the feeling that you have matched or exceeded the life built by your parents—is an important part of most people's well-being. Author Jennifer Breheny Wallace writes: "The parent-child bond is the most important relationship for a child's mental health. When a child cannot meet a parent's high expectations, that bond becomes jeopardized."

Find your own way—I don't judge—but consider these points and pick your lifestyle carefully.

Once your kids are grown, stable, and on their own, my philosophies of handling kids and money adapt.

When they're older, I want to use my money to be a last-resort safety net for my kids, but never as a fuel. So much of success in life is learning how to fail without failing so hard you can't recover. I want to prevent collapse. But I never want to use money as a crutch for my kids to avoid learning—on their own—the values of hard work, dignity, and managing failure.

Here's how I put it in a letter to my kids:

> This may sound harsh, but I hope you're poor at some point. Not struggling, and not unhappy, of course. But there's no way to learn the value of money without feeling the power of its scarcity.
>
> Your parents will work hard to support you and open the doors of opportunity. But we're not going to spoil you. We're not trying to be mean. Learning that you can't have everything you want is the only way to understand the difference between a need and a desire. It will teach you how to budget, how to save, and how to value what you already have. Learning to be frugal without it hurting is an essential life skill that will come in handy during life's inevitable ups and downs.

Author Rob Henderson makes a related point that's stuck with me. A noble goal as a parent should not be to raise successful children—success should be an offshoot of raising children who feel confident enough to find success on their own. He writes:

> I've come to believe that upward social mobility shouldn't be our priority as a society. Rather, upward mobility should be the side effect of far

more important things: family, stability, and emotional security for children.

I tell my kids that true success is when the people who you want to love you do love you. And that love comes overwhelmingly from how you treat people, rather than what you spend or a level of net worth. The most important financial advice I can give to my kids is that money alone won't provide the thing that they and almost everyone want most in life. No amount of money can compensate for a lack of character, honesty, and genuine empathy toward others.

When I think of it like that, it's so obvious what I want to teach them: the character, psychology, and attitude needed to be confident workers, trusted friends, and good citizens, which in turn will help them thrive financially.

A few other things about money and kids I've always found important:

1. Warren Buffett says it's good to have people in your life who you don't want to disappoint.

There may be no better example of this than having kids.

It's common for parents to ask how their money will influence their children, but the reverse is often as meaningful. How do your children influence your financial decisions?

Financial advisor Carl Richards says the point of a good financial advisor is to "put a gap between you and stupid." To guard against your worst impulses. Having kids in your life who you don't want to disappoint can do that in such a powerful way.

Which leads to the next point.

2. Your kids are paying attention.

Always, and all the time. Whether you realize it or not.

If the parents are spoiled and materialistic, the kids will be too. If the parents are hardworking with good values, watch what happens to the kids.

There are several studies showing kids inherit most of their political beliefs from their parents. One Pew study showed that eight in ten parents who lean Republican had teens who identify as Republican; for Democrats, it's nine in ten.

What I think is remarkable about those numbers is that most parents don't sit their kids down to intentionally explain why one political party is better than the other. There's almost never a detailed, explicit lecture of pros and cons, counters and rebuttals. But the kids still inherit the views because they're always paying attention. They notice the offhand comments, the winces while watching the news, how the parent responds to this election or that neighbor's opinion. Over time, through the accumulation of thousands of subtle clues—few of which the parent meant to be explicit— the child builds up what become firm political beliefs.

Money can be so similar.

You don't have to sit your kids down at the dinner table and explain your money values to them. They already know. Since they were small children they have cataloged every time you said, "We can't afford that" or "I love that we bought this." They see what you value. They watch what you waste. They made a mental note of how happy you were when you came home and announced that you got a raise, or how scared you looked when you got laid off. They noticed when you were envious of your neighbor's new car. They heard you and your spouse bickering over spending decisions. They noticed when you were greedy. They noticed when you were frugal.

They paid attention to all of it. And by the time they're adults, it will have accumulated into a profound effect on how they think about money.

3. What do you want them to pay attention to?

When you realize kids are always paying attention, you realize that every moment is an opportunity to lead by example.

I want to show my kids how you can use money as a tool to live a better life. I do not want to burden—or even poison—them with displays of insecurity and greed.

I want to show, by example, that if you've already covered what matters in terms of family, health, and friends, you feel less desire to use your money to show off for strangers.

I want to show, by example, that no amount of money you have, and no material item you possess, will cause people to like you if you're also a jerk, lack empathy, or feel superior to those who haven't been as fortunate as you.

I want to show, by example, that the highest use of money is to use it to control your time, granting freedom and independence, and living life the way you choose.

4. Remember what they'll remember you by.

Jonas Salk, inventor of the polio vaccine, was once asked what his main aim in life was.

"To be a good ancestor," he replied.

What a wonderful goal for every parent. To leave your kids, grandkids, and future generations the knowledge of how the world works, the wisdom to know what matters, the independence to make their own choices, the confidence to take risks, the prudence to be a long-term thinker, and the values to know how they themselves can become good ancestors.

How much of being a good ancestor has to do with money? Buying your kids nice things? Or leaving them an inheritance?

Ah, it's often so little.

It's easy for parents to think that spending money on their kids will lead them to a better life. But that thinking can be a crutch. It's often an excuse to avoid teaching some of the life lessons that are more meaningful and enduring, or to be there for them, or to show your love in different ways.

Kids may want your money, but what they'll come to value—and remember you by—are the deeper values that money can't buy.

SPREADSHEETS DON'T CARE
ABOUT YOUR FEELINGS

When emotions are more insightful than numbers.

My wife and I pride ourselves on making unemotional financial decisions. But a decade ago we were in the market for our first house. We found one online that we liked, and as we headed out for a tour we promised ourselves we wouldn't do anything rash—this was just gathering information.

Then we pulled into the driveway and my wife gasped, "I love it!" I did too. We had an infant son—our first—and there was a kids' tree swing in the front yard. Perfect.

And that was it. Emotion was involved and there was nothing we could do about it.

In a perfect world, the decision to buy a home would be a calm analysis made on a spreadsheet. In reality, you walk through a for-sale house and imagine where furniture will go. You picture Christmas morning with your kids and dream about barbecues with your friends.

The night before our bid was accepted I asked my wife how she'd feel if we lost the house. "I'd be devastated," she said. I would have been too. I know this is an awful way to think about the biggest financial decision of your life, but it was the reality of the moment. It's the reality of what almost everyone does. No one thinks about buying a home the same way they think about buying a toaster.

We have zero regrets—the house really was great. But no one should pretend that you can make life-changing decisions that will massively impact you and your family and treat it like a math problem you can solve in a spreadsheet. Spreadsheets don't care about your feelings. But sometimes those feelings are the most important part of a big financial decision.

The important thing here is realizing that not all emotional financial decisions are reckless. Many of them are profoundly important. Jason Zweig of *The Wall Street Journal* once wrote about his mom selling her longtime home:

> "I have no emotional attachment to the house; I never liked it physically," Mom told us. "But everything important that ever happened in our life as a family is here, and I can't just leave all that behind."

If I said, "How much are the memories with your kids worth?" you'd say it's impossible to attach a dollar figure. But if I said, "What is the fair market value of the home where you formed memories with your kids?" you could probably spit out a dollar figure with ease.

Understanding the difference between those two helps explain a lot of spending decisions.

Who do you think finds a better spouse: the person who makes a spreadsheet of characteristics they demand and only considers someone who checks every box, or one who seren-dipitously meets a partner and knows in their heart that things just seem to click?

In truth, the best decisions probably happen at the inter-section of the two—head and heart. The sweet spot with money is someone who is driven by equal parts rational math and emotional joy. You want to be responsible with numbers but also know how to make the numbers work for your soul.

But since money looks like a math-based field, too many people trip over themselves viewing financial problems solely through the lens of what's rational, what's efficient, and what's methodical.

Louis Armstrong, the greatest jazz musician of all time, was once asked what makes good music. "If it sounds good, you don't worry what it is," he said. "Just go and enjoy it. Anything you can tap your foot to is good music."

So many things work like that.

How do you find music you enjoy? Or food you love? How do you value the memories you'll make in a home you love?

You don't consult the rational part of your brain. The subjective, emotional part is not only in control—it *should be* in control. It knows what you want better than the spread-sheets ever could.

I actually think managing money becomes easier when you come to terms with how emotional it can be. Instead of a math problem to solve, you view it as an emotional problem to fulfill, within the confines of some budgetary boundaries.

A couple more words about those boundaries in the next chapter.

THE FINER THINGS

The wisdom, and futility, of obsessing over small purchases.

Author Rory Sutherland writes, "The opposite of a good idea can also be a good idea."

With that in mind, let's discuss the topic of obsessing over small expenses in your budget. I want to convince you that doing so can be life-changing and, also, a complete waste of time.

Former President Calvin Coolidge was notoriously frugal. Taking command over a federal budget that spent $21 billion during this term, Coolidge's team once sent a card to every clerk at the Department of Agriculture that read:

> Government Correspondence Costs
> *26¢ per letter.* Help Reduce the Cost.
> Write Fewer Letters. Write Briefer Letters.

To make letter-writing even more precarious, Coolidge's official policy was that each government employee be issued one pencil at a time, and if the pencil was not used down to its eraser, it was to be returned to the government for further use.

Do you find this absurd? Well, consider that the federal government employed roughly 585,000 people in 1925. If each wrote five letters per day—remember, this was before email and was just the early days of widespread telephone use—a $0.26 letter cost the government more than $197 million per year. This was during a time when all government spending was roughly $2.8 billion per year.

That's almost 7 percent of government spending on *letters*.

Let me give you some context: In 2023 the federal government spent approximately 10 percent of its budget on interest on the national debt.

These are not small numbers. Coolidge was not an idiot.

Author Kevin Kelly writes, "Tend to the small things. More people are defeated by blisters than mountains."

Let me give you a crazier example.

John D. Rockefeller was once discussing soldering caps onto oil cans with the plant's resident expert.

"How many drops of solder do you use on each can?"

"Forty," the man replied.

"Have you ever tried thirty-eight?" Rockefeller asked. "No? Would you mind having some sealed with thirty-eight and let me know?"

Thirty-eight drops wasn't enough—the cans leaked. But thirty-nine seemed to work fine. It became the new norm. One drop less than the original forty-drop standard.

"That one drop of solder," Rockefeller later said, "saved

$2,500 the first year; but the export business kept on increasing after that and doubled, quadrupled—became immensely greater than it was then; and the saving has gone steadily along, one drop on each can, and has amounted since to many hundreds of thousands of dollars."

That's something like $20 million in today's dollars.

The point is that small changes at scale yield massive impact.

It's common to find someone who bought their home in, say, 1974, for something like $60,000. Today it's worth perhaps $350,000. The owners no doubt feel they have made a bonanza investment.

But those numbers equate to an average annual return of 3.75 percent. Property taxes tend to average roughly 1 percent, so that brings our real return to 2.75 percent per year. Maintenance and repairs vary greatly, but spending 1 to 3 percent of your home's value per year on upkeep should be expected.

Where does that leave our long-term returns? Ah, quite dim.

The small, easy-to-ignore expenses add up to be so profound over time that they overwhelm the large, obvious costs you pay the most attention to.

Price is easy to calculate. It's just whatever you paid initially and sold for eventually. Cost is harder to figure out, because it tends to be a slow drip over time, which is easy to ignore but adds up quickly. Same for cars, boats, and hobbies. You can even say the cost of smoking cigarettes is the price of a pack plus the long-term cost of medical care associated with the habit. One is easy to calculate, the other is very difficult.

I once heard this story. A man notices his co-worker drinking a latte. He asks, "How often do you drink lattes?"

"Every day," says the coworker.

"Wow! Every day for thirty years of your professional career!" says the man. "That's so much money! A latte a day means you're spending about $1,900 a year. If you invested that money instead at an eight percent return, you'd have $250,000. That's enough to buy a Ferrari."

The coworker looks puzzled.

"Do you buy lattes?" she asked the man.

"No."

"So where's your Ferrari?"

Now, please, if you enjoy lattes, buy them all day long. The point here is that almost everyone has small expenses that could have added up to a fortune if they were tended to more carefully. And they could have been tended to with so little effort—a few bucks here, a couple bucks there. People expend enormous effort improving their investment returns because they know if you can improve your annual returns by even 0.1 percent per year, it can add up to a fortune when compounded over time. But when it comes to little expenses—letters, solder, lattes—that logic is harder to grasp.

Warren Buffett was so obsessed with compounding at an early age that he measured current expenses by what that amount would be worth in the future if he instead invested it and let it grow. A haircut, in his mind, cost $30,000—that's what the few bucks would be worth in the future if he instead let it compound. An expensive suit cost millions in forgone future investment returns. A car wash wasn't worth it under this logic; it would cost tens of thousands of dollars in future money to remove some dirt. "I'm not sure I want to blow $500,000 that way," Buffett would tell friends when pondering whether to spend a few bucks.

Chris Davis tells a story about being in New York as a kid and asking his grandfather for a $1 hot dog. His grandfather said that if he could earn the same investment returns he had earned over his life, that $1 hot dog actually cost *$1,000.* (Chris recently did the actual math and found his grandfather wasn't exaggerating; his grandfather Shelby Davis grew his assets many hundreds of times during his lifetime.)

You might find this behavior miserly. I would not recommend it to ordinary people (please eat when you're hungry and cut your hair when you feel like it).

The point is that when you understand how quickly small expenses compound into enormous lost returns, you view the world differently. You realize that building a long-term fortune has less to do with big, brilliant decisions and more to do with small, consistent decisions compounded over a long period of time.

Now, let me provide the opposite view, which I hope you'll find just as persuasive.

There's a saying I love: Save a little bit of money each month, and at the end of the year you'll be surprised at how little you still have.

Historian Cyril Northcote Parkinson coined a thing called Parkinson's Law of Triviality. It states: "The amount of attention a problem gets is the inverse of its importance."

Parkinson described a fictional finance committee with three tasks: approval of a $10 million nuclear reactor, $400 for an employee bike shed, and $20 for employee refreshments in the break room.

The committee approves the $10 million nuclear reactor immediately, because the number is too big to contextualize, alternatives are too daunting to consider, and no one on the committee is an expert in nuclear power.

The bike shed gets considerably more debate. Committee members argue whether a bike rack would suffice and whether a shed should be wood or aluminum, because they have some experience working with those materials at home.

Employee refreshments take up two thirds of the debate, because everyone has a strong opinion on what's the best coffee, the best cookies, the best chips, etc.

Many households operate the same.

Author Ramit Sethi says too many people ask $3 questions (can I afford this latte?) when all that matters to financial success are $30,000 questions (what college should I go to?).

The latte example I use above often drives financial advisors mad, because they see people wondering if they should cut lattes from their budget when those same people attend colleges they can't afford, own cars they can't afford, and live in homes they can't afford. They obsess over $3 problems while $300,000 problems get far less attention.

The amount of attention a problem gets is the inverse of its importance.

I think part of the reason this happens is because focusing on small-budget items makes you feel like you're being responsible, taking action, and making progress, which makes it easier to ignore the big problems. People can recognize when they're being oblivious, giving zero attention to a problem. But when you can say, "Look at me, cutting lattes from my budget like a responsible budgeter," it's harder to recognize that you're being irresponsible with much larger purchases.

For the vast majority of people, a handful of budget items make up the vast majority of expenses:

- College
- Home
- Car
- Health insurance
- Childcare

That's it. That's what should get all your attention. Everything else is a rounding error.

Tending to small expenses can compound into a fortune. They can also suck your attention away from much larger problems.

I don't think these two points contradict each other. Remember, the opposite of a good idea can also be a good idea. They are equally important.

A lot of doing well with money is understanding the barbell approach to good behavior.

Save like a pessimist and invest like an optimist.

Expect the worst, hope for the best.

Live for today, prepare for tomorrow.

Let me offer another: It's almost impossible to build wealth without controlling your biggest expenses. And it's very difficult to grow wealth without caring about smaller expenses.

Now let's talk about greed and fear.

THE LIFE CYCLE OF
GREED AND FEAR

*It begins innocent, turns crazy, and ends up
right where you began.*

*Some she at once crushes beneath her cruel feet;
others she condemns to a fate like that of galley slaves;
a few she favors and fondles, riding them high on the bubbles
   of fortune;
then with a sudden breath she blows the bubbles out and
   laughs mockingly as she watches them fall.*

—JAMES WELDON JOHNSON ON NEW YORK CITY

Greed and fear control so much in life.

I think of it like this: There is no amount of success that can't be destroyed by the temptation to grab too much of it. And there is no opportunity so appealing that it will catch the eye of someone who refuses to look.

These two innocent emotions are the root cause of most money mistakes, regrets, and embarrassments.

Greed and fear are everywhere you look in money, and not just how we invest our money, or the booms and busts of markets. They can be central to how we spend money too.

Spending money often requires optimism; saving often requires pessimism. At one level, both of those emotions are not only OK, they are necessary and useful. At another level, they backfire and turn into dangerous liabilities. You often only know when you've crossed the line when it's too late. So much of success in life is finding the delicate balance of when optimism turns into greed and pessimism turns into fear.

And greed and fear are sneaky. People with the best intentions and ethics get sucked into their trap. While you might think of them as opposites, they share a common origin. There is a natural cycle that causes innocent optimism to evolve into greed, which turns into denial, then confusion, then, eventually, fear. It often drops you off where you began, with the lesson you think you learned from experiencing fear setting up your next rendezvous with greed.

Understanding how powerful and dangerous these two emotions can be requires appreciating the cycle that causes them in the first place.

Here's how it happens.

All greed begins with the most innocent idea: that you deserve to be right.

The decisions you've made in the past. The decisions you'll make in the future. The worldview you hold today. It's hard to wake up in the morning and look in the mirror without telling yourself that you've made good decisions in the past and you will continue making them in the future. Nothing would get done if people doubted themselves all day. This is especially true if you've had past success in education and work.

And you *deserve* to be right because you've put so much effort into developing your views and decisions.

Maybe you went to school for years. You passed hard tests. You dealt with bullies. You did hard thinking and put in long hours. No one wants to hear they went through that grind and still don't deserve to be right.

And deserving to be right means you should be rewarded for being right. Effort equals reward. That's how the world works, isn't it?

If you have accurate views, you'll make good decisions, and those decisions will be rewarded by your peers with admiration, your bosses with pay raises, and your body with health.

It's such an appealing, attractive thought.

It's hard to make it through the day admitting you don't know how the world works. So almost no one does it. We tell ourselves that our beliefs are correct, and correct views will be rewarded.

The conviction that whatever you believe is right, and you deserve to be right because you've put in so much effort to form those beliefs, and correct beliefs will be rewarded by the world, is such a common and innocent idea.

And it's where things start to get messy.

When you are rewarded for being right, a door opens inside your head that invites delusion to step inside.

Recognition feels good. Attention feels good. Rewards feel good. They're addictive. It gets back to the first innocent idea: People want to feel like they're right, doing well, and owed something for their efforts.

195

In a rational world, we'd try to calculate how much of what we did influenced the reward we received. We'd recognize that if you did *this* and then *that* happened, there are a million other variables you have no control over that also could have influenced *that* outcome.

But that's not a natural way to think.

The default assumption when you're rewarded for doing something is to assume that you doing *this* caused *that* to happen. If you're looking for an answer to why *that* happened, it is the path of least resistance.

Because, after all, your views are right and deserve to be rewarded. So of course the reward was caused by the thing you did.

Others believe this as much as you.

People watch you get a reward and—because they imagine how they would feel if they got a reward—they get excited by your achievement. Praise. Attention. Admiration. And yes, jealousy and envy. It all feels good to you, and reinforces the idea that you got rewarded because your views and actions were right.

And you want more of it.

Success makes it easy to say, "I was right before, so now I'm going to double down."

It's not a crazy thought. It's part reasonable analysis; you tested the waters and were proven right, so now dive in. And it's part social comparison; the buzz you got from being a little right wore off. Now you want to be right in a bigger way.

This is an important part of greed: People justify their actions, even when in hindsight those actions were clearly excessive or crazy. It's different than knowing your actions are reckless and harmful but doing them anyway. That's psychopathy. The common form of innocent greed is extrapolating with enthusiasm what worked in the past.

It tempts you to do the same thing as before, but with twice the appetite.

Maybe you have the same job, but you demand more pay. You have the same investments, but now with leverage. Or you got some attention for the new car and, eager for more, you now want the new watch, clothes, jewelry, and house.

This may be fine to do if your actions directly influence outcomes. If doing *this* causes *that*.

But if your previous actions aren't sustainable, or if you underestimate how much of your previous outcomes were caused by actions that weren't in your control, then doubling down on what worked in the past increases the odds that doing more isn't going to end well.

Greed happens when you double down on actions that at one time worked but aren't sustainable, or that cause you to overestimate how influential your actions were on outcomes.

Maybe you underestimate how much of your past success was luck, randomness, or being in the right place at the right time.

Maybe the people who in the past rewarded you with attention are no longer around.

Maybe people who were excited for your past success are now exhausted from hearing about you.

Perhaps your boss who was happy to reward you for your

past contributions is now tired of you demanding yet another raise.

People who used to give you attention now snicker at you.

Whatever the cause, sometimes the world views your actions as a taunt, and reality creeps in to remind you that things are more complicated than you assumed.

What worked in the past suddenly doesn't work anymore. But since your whole strategy has been to believe that you're right, deserve to be rewarded for being right, and are doubling down on what used to work, now you're in trouble.

Peak greed is expecting to get back more than you deserve given what you put in. Which is exactly what happens when you overestimate your ability to do things that will directly lead to rewards.

You don't know it yet, but the seeds of fear have been planted.

The first reaction to greed backfiring is to view it as an opportunity, especially when you're blinded to the realities of your skill and contributions.

When the strategy that used to reward you stops working, you cut off those who go against you, and maybe double down on your actions yet again.

If a novice with no record of success experiences a loss or a failure, they are likely to take it as a signal that they have no skill and no idea what they're doing.

But if you mistakenly think your skill has been confirmed to the point where you've become greedy, experiencing a loss is often interpreted as the world giving you a new opportunity.

"The company denied my raise, so now I can find a new job at a place that appreciates me."

"My friends don't appreciate my fancy things, so I'll go find new people who do."

"You don't praise me for my car anymore, maybe I need a new, better one."

You will rarely find this mindset in someone who hasn't experienced past success. It only comes from someone who's convinced that their past actions have caused their past results.

Their response is often to double down yet again, with even more confidence.

When you've overestimated how much of your actions influence your results, you miss key feedback the world tries to give you, sticking to your guns instead of updating your approach. You keep plugging ahead, which seems like an admirable trait. You may throw more effort at the strategy, convinced it will pay off with even bigger rewards when you're eventually proven right.

You think you're being determined, but you're actually being stubborn.

Buddhism has a concept called Beginner's Mind, which is an active openness to trying new things and studying new ideas, unburdened by past preconceptions, like a beginner would. Assuming you have skill can be the enemy of a beginner's mind, because past success reduces the incentive to explore other ideas, especially when those ideas conflict with your proven strategy. It's dangerous. Being locked into a single view is fatal in an economy where reversion to the mean and competition constantly dismantle old strategies.

When you give up a flexible mind, you are now immune to feedback. So now you are less prepared than a beginner, or even someone attempting random strategies in the dark.

The odds of your continued failure now escalate.

After multiple failures, you begin to view yourself as a victim.

You have not yet admitted the possibility that perhaps you were never as skilled as you once imagined, even to yourself.

You see the world as acting against you.

You blame your friends.

You blame your boss.

You blame the media.

You blame politicians.

You become angry at others.

Anything but looking in the mirror.

At this point, greed is dead, but denial about your contributions and skill is at its highest.

You try to reduce risk without abandoning ship. You cut back on your actions a little, maybe apologize to those you offended.

You have not given up hope. But you recognize you need a change and are confident you can get back on track.

At this point, you have admitted to yourself that you engaged in excess. But you still haven't admitted you were wrong. The problem, in your mind, is that you pushed too much of a good thing. But that thing still looks good. It's still right. It still deserves to be rewarded.

So you carry on, with just a little less enthusiasm than before.

You can only maintain delusion for so long. You eventually start to give up on your actions.

Sometimes it takes days for that to happen, sometimes years. But it will happen.

And it is the point where you start to wonder whether you've missed something along the way.

You don't yet realize you were wrong. Admitting you were wrong is *painful*. But—perhaps—you realize your views were incomplete.

This is when people start saying things like "We've learned a lot in the last year" and "This has been a growth experience."

Sometimes these statements are honest and correct. But often they are just a bare-bones way of signaling to others you have not completely lost touch with reality. Deep down, your core views and faith in your ability are still mostly intact.

There comes a point where it's obvious, even to you, that you are wrong. Privately, to yourself, you wonder whether you were wrong. On occasion you admit to others that, yes, you were.

To deal with the pain you often employ denial. When friends ask you how things are going, you change the subject, nearly to the point of denying you were ever involved with the thing you once went all in on. "It was never that important to me," or "It was always a small part of what I enjoy."

Reality rushes in when your mistakes force lifestyle changes. When you're forced to sell your house or your car, or cancel a vacation, or move into a smaller office, the consequences of your wrongness are now undeniable to anyone watching you.

Now you're embarrassed.

And once you're embarrassed, your ability to look at a problem with a cool, rational mind becomes as clouded as it was when you were in the peak of greed.

A little doubt that you were wrong now cascades into panic.

You avoid people you'd normally talk to about your skill, which walls you off even more from the ability to take feedback and gain context on your situation. You're now stuck in your own mind, which becomes a doom loop of fear and doubt.

Your mindset shifts from growth to damage control. You stop thinking about opportunity and gain. Your definition of success is now when you stop falling behind.

Anything that prevents further loss now looks like an appealing gain.

So you sell what you have left. Leave your career. Sell your car. Abandon your company. It feels like capitulation.

When you were greedy you believed that 100 percent of what you did influenced the gains you received. Now you think there's nothing you can do that's in your control that will deliver upside.

The hard thing is, you're as wrong now as you were back then. But you're equally blind to that reality.

You begin looking around at everyone else. The people you once looked down upon now sit so much higher than you. What happened? Why aren't they suffering like you? Do they know something you don't?

That's a new fear to worry about.

When you were successful, people watched what you were doing and tried to copy it. They wondered what you knew that they didn't. They didn't want to miss the rewards you were getting.

Now the process goes in the other direction. You start looking at other people who have done better than you and wonder what else they know that you don't.

But since you're now gripped with fear, you're not looking for upside opportunities. You wonder what other landmines exist that smarter people have avoided but you might still be oblivious to.

Fear does the most damage when your biggest fear is wondering what else you should be fearful about.

You become as blind to what positive things might happen as you were to what negative things might happen when you were greedy.

The irony is that chaos is often the most fertile ground for opportunity and a chance to go in a different direction. But opportunity is the last thing you're now thinking about. You're focused on not falling down any further.

At some point you find stabilization. People begin to forgive you. Fear gives way to acceptance. You find a new groove. You lost a lot of what you once had, but now you can think with a clearer head.

The first thing you vow is to never make the same mistake again.

The pain you went through with fear was ten times harder than the joy you got from greed. If there's a silver lining from this debacle, it's that you've learned your lesson and can avoid the same errors in the future.

You now have a new worldview. A new strategy on how to operate in markets, business, and life, shaped by the mistakes you made when you fell for the trap of greed and fear. You now know how to act when opportunity presents itself.

You feel confident about this new view. You deserve to be smarter now. Going through something as hard as you've been through and not coming away smarter seems unfair. You were wrong before, but now you're right. No one wants to hear they went through that painful grind and still don't deserve to be right.

And deserving to be right means you should be rewarded for being right. Effort equals reward. That's how the world works, isn't it?

It's hard to wake up in the morning and look in the mirror without telling yourself that you can make good decisions.

Isn't that an innocent view?

That you deserve to be right?

And now we're right back to where this story began.

HOW TO BE MISERABLE
SPENDING YOUR MONEY

A brief guide to bad decisions.

A n important fact of life is that it's often difficult to know what will make you happy, but quite easy to identify what will make you miserable.

When faced with a difficult problem—and how to spend money in a way that will improve your life certainly is—it can help to work backward, reducing and excluding what doesn't work until what's left over is a decent approximation of favorable traits. Evolution works in similar ways, so thoroughly destroying what doesn't work that what's left over tends to work quite well. Or think about health: What foods are good for you is an endless debate, and no one who's honest with the evidence can say they know the perfect diet. But what's *bad* for you is much more settled. I have no idea if a glass of red wine is good for me. I am 100 percent sure that cigarettes are not.

A young boy once asked Charlie Munger, "What advice do you have for someone like me to succeed in life?" Munger replied: "Don't do cocaine. Don't race trains to the track. And avoid all AIDS situations." Succeed by first knowing what to avoid.

In the same way, I can't tell you how to spend money,

because I'm not you. And I can't tell you what will make you happy, because I'm still trying to figure that out for myself. Everyone's different and life is complex. But what leads to a miserable life tends to be universal and straightforward.

So let me offer you a brief guide on how to be miserable with your money.

Direct your gaze at the socioeconomic group just above you, assuming that within it you will find a level of durable happiness. Tell yourself that you'll be satisfied once you make just a little more money, have a little bit nicer home, and can spend just a little bit more than you do now. Ignore the fact that the group you're in now used to be a dream that you thought would bring you contentment and happiness.

Pursue status at the expense of independence. Assume that happiness relies on masses of strangers being impressed by the material possessions you own rather than the hidden magic of you owning your own time.

Let money—the making of it, the spending of it, the accumulation of it—become a core part of your identity. Spend more time thinking about money than the life you've built with that money.

Spend so much of your income that you become completely reliant on the decisions of other people, like bosses and bankers, many of whom couldn't care less about you.

Fantasize that having more money is the solution to all your problems. Tell yourself that you'd wake up every morning with a smile on your face if you had just a little more money. Imagine that you'd be more liked, more admired, you'd have more friends and healthier relationships. Believe that none of your current fears, anxieties, doubts, and confusions in life would exist if only you had more money than you do now.

Assume money can solve none of your problems, and that it is the root of evil and ego. This can be just as dangerous as the previous point. Money is a remarkable tool, capable of offering independence and the joys that come from thousands of years of humans figuring out how to make life more comfortable, entertaining, and enlightening. How tragic it is to live in a world where you believe the accumulated efforts of the one hundred billion people who came before you have produced nothing worthy of your time and attention.

Have such a fierce saving ideology that you're never able to treat yourself to a good life you can afford. Act like money's only purpose is to accumulate in your bank account, where instead of a tool to live a better life you've essentially formed an accounting hobby.

When taking stock of your own life, assume that all your success is due to hard work and all your failure is due to bad luck. When judging others, assume all failure is due to bad decisions and all success was due to luck. Place ego over empathy. This is the surest way to become detached from the reality of what you can and cannot control in life.

Compare your inside with other people's outside, envying others' success without having a full picture of their lives. Assume that other people's cars, homes, clothes, jewelry, and social media accounts are an accurate reflection of how happy they are. Tell yourself that because they have nice toys they must also have good relationships, good health, moral clarity, emotional intelligence, and overall life satisfaction.

Ignore the hidden social, emotional, and expectations costs that come from certain purchases. Ignore what some purchases will do to other people's impression of you. Forget that you may have created a higher bar you'll need to exceed during the next purchase, which is a hidden form of debt.

Have no sense of your own tendency to regret. Become so wrapped up in the bubble of the current moment, or so fixated on the long run, that you eventually look back at your life and wonder what the hell you were thinking.

Associate net worth with self-worth (for you and others). Think of money as the ultimate scorecard for how well people have done in life—and, worse, assume that their material appearance is an accurate indication of how much money they actually have.

Treat all financial decisions as math decisions with no appreciation for reasonable emotion, sentimental value, and desire to feed your soul. Become more interested in making the spreadsheets happy than making yourself happy.

Be persuaded by the advice and lifestyle of those who need or want something you don't. Want what society says that you should want. Desire what the marketers say you should desire. Look to other people, including strangers, for answers on what's best for you. Have no appreciation for the vast spectrum of people's needs, wants, and desires.

Anchor your lifestyle expectations to the most successful people you know, creating a mindset where even exceptional success in your own life feels inadequate. It's basically a contract with yourself to be unhappy.

Become so optimistic that your expectations grow faster than income. Live in a world where things get better but you appreciate none of it because you expected all of it, and more.

Risk what you need in order to gain what you don't need. Risk relationships with your family and friends for the potential of a raise that will have little impact on your life, or risk how well you sleep at night for a new car that no one will pay attention to.

Overestimate the attention you get from having nice stuff, and assume the attention you do get is a reflection of people admiring you versus them fantasizing about having what you have for themselves.

Assume you have all the right answers. Try nothing new. Reject the mystery of life, and fight against all inclinations you have to grow, adapt, and change your mind. Be curious of no alternative viewpoints. Assume that what you know about money is all there is to know, and argue fiercely when you discover information that might go against your current beliefs. Treat money as you might treat religion, with devotion above curiosity and orthodoxy above exploration.

You will, I guarantee, be on your way to misery. Now let me tell you how I've tried to avoid it.

THE LUCKIER YOU ARE,
THE NICER YOU SHOULD BE

My simple path to a good financial life.

Kevin Costner, one of the greatest and most successful actors of modern times, once told a story that stopped me in my tracks.

Costner had a friend—he doesn't say who, but when you piece together the details was almost certainly the author Michael Blake—who after years of writing had found little success.

"I sent him on a lot of jobs" trying to find him work, Costner said. "Every report that came back was that he pissed everyone off."

The friend pushed Costner to make introductions. "Even though every writer thinks the last thing they wrote is the best thing they wrote, maybe it's just not good enough," Costner bluntly told him.

One day the friend called Costner and said, "Hey, I don't have a place to stay, can I stay at your house?" He was homeless.

"So he stays there for a couple of months," Costner says. The whole time the friend was writing furiously. "He's writing every night. And he says, 'Will you read what I wrote today?'"

"I said no." It was like Costner thought of the friend as a stray cat to pity, not a work collaborator to admire and learn from.

"He started reading it to my daughter, who was three, every night," Costner said. "Finally my wife said, 'Look, he's got to go.' I said to him, 'Yeah, you got to go.'"

Away the friend went. He eventually found himself in Arizona, washing dishes in a Chinese restaurant.

Months later he called Costner and asked, "Did you ever read what I wrote?"

"No," Costner said.

Feeling bad, Costner sent the friend—still ostensibly homeless—a sleeping bag.

Later the friend called and asked again: "Did you ever read what I wrote?"

Annoyed, Costner relented.

"Finally I read it," Costner said.

"It was *Dances with Wolves.*"

It went on to be a blockbuster. The film adaptation won seven Academy Awards and catapulted Costner's career into superstardom.

You never know where luck might come from in life.

More on that in a second.

———

My mom says I started counting pennies when I was three years old. I didn't want to count anything else. Just money.

Charlie Munger once said that when teaching money to

young people they either understand it instantly or never at all. I don't think it's that black and white. But when I think about my own life, I wonder. Since receiving my first pay-check as a teenager, I've saved and invested a double-digit percentage of every dollar I've made. It always just seemed like the right thing to do—I don't think anyone taught me, and it was never a challenge. It just felt obvious.

My wife and I don't spend a lot, because we don't want a lot. We live a very nice life, but most of what we value and enjoy doing doesn't cost much—hikes, gardening, reading, writing, taking our dog for a long walk, quality time with our kids, that sort of thing. The amount of income we've earned over the years has changed dramatically, but what we enjoy has not.

We would love each other just as much if we were poor— and indeed we did—but we've used the money we've saved over the years to become independent, and I can't describe how fulfilling that's been. To be specific: My wife became a stay-at-home mom, and I pick and choose the work that seems interesting to me and reject the rest, valuing inde-pendence over income at every turn. Both of those decisions have a financial component, but neither felt like rejecting money as much as purchasing time.

My only financial goal is to go to bed every night with a sense of calm, knowing my family is OK and that I can spend the next day doing what I want, when I want, with whom I want, for as long as I want. Beating the stock market has no appeal to me. Impressing my neighbors has never crossed my mind. Those seem like external-benchmark goals, where victory is not defined by how well you're doing but merely by whether you're doing better than random strangers. It always seemed like a pointless game to me. Independence offers the highest ROI that money can buy, and I don't think it's even close.

Our financial life is so simple. My wife and I met in college, merged our finances soon after (before we married), and we really don't talk about money that much because there's not much to discuss. There are no budgets, no detailed spreadsheets, no elaborate strategies or arbitrary targets. Our entire net worth is a house, cash, index funds, and shares of Markel Group where I'm on the board of directors. We have no debt at all. We buy just about anything we want, but since we don't want much it's never been an issue. That was true when we made next to nothing and it's been true during our highest-income years. We've also experimented with so many different lifestyle spending choices over the years that we're confident we're not depriving ourselves of enjoyment for the sake of saving more.

It hasn't been perfect. I've made bad investments, dumb decisions, and like most parents my wife and I wonder whether we're passing along the right financial values to our kids. No one can recognize how many different ways there are to live a life and how imperfect they are and honestly say they're doing everything right. I've also changed my mind about plenty over the years. And the right lesson from changing your mind is wondering which other of your beliefs you'll eventually update.

When you accept how messy money can be, you value

good-enough simplicity over the false comfort of complexity. Over the years I've come up with a few simple thoughts that guide how I think about money in my own house.

Spend less than you make.

Quietly compound.

Money serves you, not the other way around.

No one is thinking about you as much as you are.

Independence is wealth.

Health is wealth.

Aim to be a good ancestor.

Love your family.

That's a pretty comprehensive list.

Now, back to Kevin Costner.

———

Benjamin Franklin didn't say honesty is the best morals—he said it's the best policy. It's what's going to help you and put you in the best position, earning you the most money, in the long run.

There's a corollary there with kindness.

There are two reasons to be kind to everyone. One is moral, the other is selfish. Morally, you should do it because you're empathetic. Selfishly, you should do it because it's easy to underestimate how many people you may eventually rely on to help you, and you'll only gain their cooperation if you remain in their good graces.

Kevin Costner's story is such a good example of never realizing where help in life might come from, and how people who don't look like the picture of success might actually hold the wisdom you're looking for.

The world is unequal—always has been and always will be. Skill is unequal, so that's for the better. But the knee-jerk association between wealth and wisdom turns dangerous when you think it's absolute. We're fortunate to live in a world that's so wealthy, with so much opportunity, and so much material abundance. But it's also become easier than ever to dangerously assume that only those who dress a certain way, live a certain way, or earn a certain income are worth paying attention to.

So let me propose one last thought about money: The luckier you are, the nicer you should be.

Having money can accentuate who you are, but it can also blind you to who others are.

If you're fortunate enough to live in a prosperous region, in a prosperous era, surrounded by the ability to learn about the world and express who you are—a beneficiary of the accumulated efforts and wisdom of the one hundred billion people who came before you—the more you should go out of your way to appreciate what money can't buy.

Realize that having money might highlight or magnify an incredible life, but it cannot create it on its own.

Understand that people who have made different decisions than you, and ended up with a different outcome than you, can be just as smart, funny, insightful, and worthy as you. They do what makes sense to them, and they're trying to find their way in a complex world. You do what makes sense to you, and you're trying to find your way in a complex world.

And so we end right where we began, with a reminder that all behavior makes sense with enough information, and we are all on our own quest for the simple life.

Acknowledgments

Like all books, *The Art of Spending Money* wouldn't have been possible without the countless people who helped me along the way. There are too many to list them all. But a few who have been particularly supportive:

Gretchen, Miles, and Reese, whose love and support is unwavering.

Brian Richards, who bet on me before anyone else.

Craig Shapiro, who bet on me when he didn't have to.

Jenna Abdou, who helps while asking for nothing in return.

Noah Schwartzberg, Mollie Glick, and Adrian Zackheim, who made this whole book happen.

Craig Pearce, who encourages, guides, and grounds me.

Plus the constant feedback and encouragement from Chris Hill, Doug Boneparth, Michael Antonelli, David Senra, and so many others.

Thank you.

Notes

Introduction: The Quest of the Simple Life

xi **ruined her life:** Robert Kurson, *Crashing Through: A True Story of Risk, Adventure, and the Man Who Dared to See* (Random House, 2007), 49.

xvi **listed them off:** Gretchen Rubin, "Carl Jung's Five Key Elements to Happiness," *Psychology Today*, February 23, 2012, psychologytoday.com/us/blog/the-happiness-project /201202/carl-jungs-five-key-elements-happiness.

xviii **"harder than knowing what to need":** Luke Burgis, *Wanting: The Power of Mimetic Desire in Everyday Life* (St. Martin's Press, 2021).

xix **"selling himself a slave to it":** "Benjamin Franklin," *The Historian's Hut* (blog), July 20, 2018, thehistorianshut.com /2018/07/20/benjamin-franklin-17.

All Behavior Makes Sense with Enough Information

3 **syndicated columnist Robert Quillen:** *The Wilkes-Barre Record*, June 28, 1928.

4 **Allen wrote about the era:** Frederick Lewis Allen, *Only Yesterday: An Informal History of the 1920s* (Harper & Brothers, 1931).

5 **"post-traumatic broke syndrome":** Charlotte Cowles, "How to Run a Multimillion-Dollar Business and Still Nap Every Day," *The Cut*, January 1, 2024, thecut.com/article/how -tiffany-aliche-gets-it-done.html.

6 **software engineer Billy Markus says:** Billy Markus (@BillyM2k), "always remember that humans are not rational, we are rationalizing; thus all of us strongly believe all sorts of stuff that isn't true and that would be quite difficult to convince us otherwise no matter the facts and evidence," X, February 13, 2024, x.com/BillyM2k/status /1757537741473226925.

7 **"by your brain as you need them":** "Cartoon Science (How Emotions Are Made)," posted February 21, 2017, by Lisa Feldman Barrett, YouTube, youtube.com/watch?v=K _rjOY0kdII.

8 **Concepts like "Anger" and "Disgust":** Lisa Feldman Barrett, *How Emotions Are Made: The Secret Life of the Brain,* (Mariner Books, 2017).

8 **by other cultures:** Jonathan Haidt, *The Righteous Mind: Why Good People Are Divided by Politics and Religion* (Vintage, 2013), 18–19.

9 **"consensus realities are mostly the result of geography":** David McRaney, *How Minds Change: The Surprising Science of Belief, Opinion, and Persuasion* (Portfolio, 2022).

9 **Take an extreme example from:** Rob Henderson, "'Luxury Beliefs' That Only the Privileged Can Afford," *Wall Street Journal,* February 9, 2024, wsj.com/us-news/education /luxury-beliefs-that-only-the-privileged-can-afford-7f6b8a16.

11 **says financial advisor Tim Maurer:** Tim Maurer, "Personal Finance Is More PERSONAL Than It Is FINANCE," Financial Life Planning, November 16, 2011, timmaurer .com/p/personal-finance-is-more-personal.

12 **Comedian George Carlin:** "George Carlin—Idiot and Maniac," youtube.com/watch?v=XWPCE2tTLZQ.

May I Have Your Attention Please

17 **Adam Smith wrote in 1759:** Adam Smith, *The Theory of Moral Sentiments* (1759), chap. 2, available at knarf.english .upenn.edu/Smith/tms132.html.

20 **for your talents alone:** Shannon Sharpe (@ShannonSharpe), ".@ochocinco saved 83% of his salary by flying Spirit &

wearing fake jewelry," X, January 30, 2023, x.com
/ShannonSharpe/status/1620223077702586370.

20 **drive a Honda Accord:** "Jeff Bezos: Old Honda?," posted
September 1, 2023, by Way, YouTube, youtube.com
/watch?v=tc0a28KrWKo.

20 **$500 million yacht:** Sarah Jackson, "Jeff Bezos' Yacht
Reportedly Cost $500 Million and Is the Largest Sailing
Yacht in the World. Here's What We Know," *Business Insider*,
November 14, 2023, businessinsider.com/jeff-bezos-yacht.

20 **didn't have any furniture:** John Brownlee, "Steve Jobs's
Quest for Perfection Could Make Even Buying a Sofa into
a Decade-Long Ordeal," *Cult of Mac*, October 25, 2011,
cultofmac.com/125861/steve-jobss-quest-for-perfection
-could-make-even-buying-a-sofa-into-a-decade-long
-ordeal.

21 **and to abuse alcohol:** Jennifer Breheny Wallace, *Never
Enough: When Achievement Culture Becomes Toxic—and
What We Can Do About It* (Portfolio, 2023), 121.

24 **"lowest of human character traits":** Jan-Willem van der Rijt,
"The Vice of Admiration," *Philosophy* 93, no. 1 (2018): 69–90,
doi.org/10.1017/S0031819117000353.

25 **"But it doesn't work":** Alice Schroeder, *The Snowball: Warren
Buffett and the Business of Life* (Bantam, 2008).

The Happiest People I Know

28 **"When you walk around":** Nina Norman, "Summary: How
Proust Can Change Your Life: Valuable Insights Into Living
Your Best Life by Alain de Botton," Paiminy, December 10,
2023, paminy.com/book-summary-how-proust-change
-your-life-valuable-insights-living-best-life.

30 **"People from a planet":** Oxford Reference, oxfordreference
.com/display/10.1093/acref/9780191826719.001.0001/q-oro
-ed4-00007730.

31 **financial advisor Peter Mallouk:** x.com/PeterMallouk.

33 **"No purpose," he said:** "The Purpose of Life Nixon,"
posted July 9, 2011, by JM, YouTube, youtube.com/watch
?v=Pc3IfB23W4c.

Everything You Don't See

37 **political rival Thomas Jefferson:** Amber Paranick, "Deaths of John Adams and Thomas Jefferson on July 4th," *Headlines & Heroes* (Library of Congress blog), July 6, 2022, blogs.loc.gov/headlinesandheroes/2022/07/deaths-of-john -adams-and-thomas-jefferson-on-july-4th.

39 **asked who he envies:** *The Solitary Billionaire: J. Paul Getty,* interview by Alan Whicker, aired February 24, 1963, on BBC, bbc.co.uk/programmes/p00nw1t5.

40 **Rubin once echoed something similar:** Patrick O'Shaughnessy (@patrick_oshag), "Rick Rubin sums up why I believe in the idea of 'growth without goals.' 'It's hard to get really depressed until your dreams come true. Once your dreams come true and you realize you feel the same way you did before then you get a feeling of hopelessness . . .'" X, August 13, 2023, x.com/patrick _oshag/status/1690759146792972288.

40 **"That's when you get hopeless":** Jay Shetty (@jayshettypodcast), "@rickrubin gets deep during our time on the podcast ⚗ If you haven't listened yet you can now on all audio platforms or you can watch on YouTube 🖥," Instagram, September 29, 2023, instagram .com/reel/CxxhghROPxF.

42 **The happiest states in America:** Jessica Roy, "Here Are the 50 States Ranked by How Happy Their Residents Are," *Time,* February 24, 2014, time.com/9465/here-are-the-50 -states-ranked-by-how-happy-their-residents-are.

42 **"things other than their disability":** Daniel Kahneman, "Focusing Illusion," n.d., response to annual question "2011: What Scientific Concept Would Improve Everybody's Cognitive Toolkit?," *Edge,* edge.org/response-detail/11984.

42 **Kahneman again (emphasis mine):** Daniel Kahneman, *Thinking, Fast and Slow* (Farrar, Straus and Giroux, 2011).

44 **"more money won't help":** Michele W. Berger, "Does More Money Correlate with Greater Happiness?," *Penn Today,* March 6, 2023, penntoday.upenn.edu/news/does-more -money-correlate-greater-happiness-Penn-Princeton -research.

45 **"how it would feel to be there":** Ben Cohen, "Taylor Swift Is Still Intimidated by the Fear of Being Average," *Wall Street Journal*, December 21, 2023, wsj.com/arts-culture/music/taylor-swift-eras-tour-success-a2358af7.

46 **"Everyone is jealous":** Jimmy Carr (@jimmycarr), X, May 29, 2024, x.com/jimmycarr/status/1796572824393703882.

46 **wrote this beautiful note:** Marc Randolph (@mbrandolph), "I'm Marc Randolph, co-founder of Netflix & 6 other companies. This is my definition of success," X, May 28, 2024, x.com/mbrandolph/status/1795468885245976631.

The Most Valuable Financial Asset Is Not Needing to Impress Anyone

50 **twenty-seven thousand miles later:** Nicholas Tomalin and Ron Hall, *The Strange Last Voyage of Donald Crowhurst* (1970; repr., International Marine/Ragged Mountain Press, 2003).

60 **"The big question about":** Alice Schroeder, *The Snowball: Warren Buffett and the Business of Life* (Bantam, 2008).

What Makes You Happy

63 **"such a carpet was happening?":** Robert Kurson, *Crashing Through: A True Story of Risk, Adventure, and the Man Who Dared to See* (Random House, 2007), 132.

65 **"The thing that is least":** *William Dawson, The Quest of the Simple Life* (E. P. Dutton and Co., 1907).

66 **Schwarzenegger once gave diet advice:** Arnold Schwarzenegger (@Schwarzenegger), "I heard that the way you go viral on this site is by making a big list of things you have to do. Let me try. You should mostly eat food you know is healthy, there is no magic food. You should also occasionally let yourself eat delicious food you know isn't healthy," X, December 18, 2023, x.com/Schwarzenegger/status/1736816475426664558.

71 **"the arrogance of wealth":** Morgan Housel, "What We Said When the World Changed," Collaborative Fund, April 5, 2017, collabfund.com/blog/what-we-said-when-the-world-changed.

The Rich and the Wealthy

75 **"any other thing that wrecked him"**: John Updike, "Poor
Little Rich Boy," *The Guardian*, June 20, 2003, theguardian
.com/books/2003/jun/21/featuresreviews.guardianreview34.

75 **the legacy of the world's richest man:** Arthur T. Vanderbilt
II, *Fortune's Children: The Fall of the House of Vanderbilt*
(William Morrow, 1989), 415.

76 **more money than the US Treasury:** David Senra
(@FoundersPodcast), "When Cornelius Vanderbilt died he
had more money than the U.S. Treasury This story is wild!
New episode available now!," X, March 11, 2024, twitter.com
/founderspodcast/status/1767302892132962454?s=43.

76 **"devote themselves to pleasure":** Vanderbilt, *Fortune's
Children.*

77 **family biographer Arthur Vanderbilt writes:** Vanderbilt,
Fortune's Children, 343.

77 **money promised to his heirs:** Vanderbilt, *Fortune's
Children*, 343.

78 **"as cocaine is to morality":** Rebecca Fowler, "'Inherited
Wealth Is a Real Handicap to Happiness. It Is as Certain a
Death to Ambition as Cocaine Is to Morality'—William K
Vanderbilt," *Independent*, July 11, 1996, independent.co.uk
/news/inherited-wealth-is-a-real-handicap-to-happiness-it
-is-as-certain-a-death-to-ambition-as-cocaine-is-to-morality
-william-k-vanderbilt-1328294.html.

79 **just "Because I can":** *The Queen of Versailles*, directed by
Lauren Greenfield (Evergreen Pictures, 2012). "Queen
of Versailles" (excerpt of transcript from *The Queen
of Versailles*), subsaga.com, n.d., subsaga.com/bbc
/documentaries/factual/storyville/2012-2013/14-queen-of
-versailles.html.

80 **in his 1926 memoir:** Harvey S. Firestone, *Men and Rubber:
The Story of Business* (1926; repr., Latticework, 2023), 26.

81 **"would have been so motivated":** Emily Burack, "Anderson
Cooper Wants to Teach His Sons the Value of Earning
a Living," *Town & Country*, September 13, 2023,
townandcountrymag.com/society/money-and-power
/a45124305/anderson-cooper-sons-inheritance.

82 **when he was newly rich:** Brian Murphy, "Charles Feeney, Philanthropist Who Gave Away His Billions, Dies at 92," *Washington Post,* October 10, 2023, washingtonpost.com /obituaries/2023/10/10/chuck-feeney-philanthropist-duty -free-dies.

82 **"isn't helping people":** "An Entrepreneur, Always," The Atlantic Philanthropies, n.d., atlanticphilanthropies.org /chuck-feeneys-story/chapter-1.

83 **Perell once wrote:** David Perell (@david_perell), "The people I admire most have a way of escaping the bubble of culture. Sometimes via religion; sometimes via old books; sometimes via time in nature. Without such an escape, propaganda wins. You stop thinking for yourself. Modern delusions grow into an all-consuming mind virus." X, November 25, 2023, twitter.com/david_perell/status /1728627591651975341.

84 **happy before you had more money:** "Kahneman Resolves Conflict on Income-Wellbeing Study, Finds Point at Which Unhappiness Stops Decreasing for Unhappy People," Kahneman-Treisman Center for Behavioral Science & Public Policy, Princeton University, press release, March 8, 2023, behavioralpolicy.princeton.edu/news/DK _wellbeing0323.

86 **"If you get to my age":** Marcel Schwantes, "Warren Buffett Says Your Greatest Measure of Success at the End of Your Life Comes Down to 1 Word," *Inc.,* September 13, 2018, inc.com/marcel-schwantes/warren-buffett-says-it-doesnt -matter-how-rich-you-are-without-this-1-thing-your-life-is -a-disaster.html.

Utility vs. Status

88 **that amounts to a religious experience:** "Sour Grapes | The World's Most Notorious Wine Forger | True Crime | FULL ENGLISH DOCUMENTARY," posted May 19, 2022, by Gravitas Documentaries, YouTube, youtube.com/watch ?v=5LGibBYuj5U.

90 **reselling the real ones online:** Amy X. Wang, "Inside the Delirious Rise of 'Superfake' Handbags," *New York Times,*

May 4, 2023, updated June 28, 2023, nytimes.com/2023/05
/04/magazine/celine-chanel-gucci-superfake-handbags
.html.

90 **Author David Brooks once wrote:** David Brooks, "The
Haimish Line," *New York Times*, August 29, 2011, nytimes
.com/2011/08/30/opinion/brooks-the-haimish-line.html.

Risk and Regret

95 **David Cassidy's last words:** Andrea Mandell, "Katie Cassidy
Shares Father David Cassidy's Last Words: 'So Much Wasted
Time,'" *USA Today*, November 24, 2017, usatoday.com/story
/life/people/2017/11/24/katie-cassidy-shares-father-david
-cassidys-last-words-so-much-wasted-time/893367001.

97 **150 years old:** J. Nielsen et al., "Eye Lens Radiocarbon
Reveals Centuries of Longevity in Greenland Shark
(*Somniosus microcephalus*)," *Science* 353, no. 6300 (2016):
702–4.

98 **Bill Perkins writes:** Bill Perkins, *Die with Zero: Getting All
You Can from Your Money and Your Life* (Mariner Books,
2020), cover flap.

99 **"Taking too little risk":** Nick Maggiulli (@dollarsanddata),
X, April 3, 2024, x.com/dollarsanddata/status/17755016774
38677460.

100 **could expect to live until age sixty-two:** Felicitie C. Bell and
Michael L. Miller, "Life Tables for the United States Social
Security Area 1900–2100," SSA Pub. No. 11-11536 (Social
Security Administration, August 2005), ssa.gov/oact
/NOTES/pdf_studies/study120.pdf.

103 **Amazon founder Jeff Bezos once described:** "Jeff Bezos—
Regret Minimization Framework," Youtube, December 20,
2008, youtube.com/watch?v=jwG_qR6XmDQ.

Look at Them

109 **"he appreciates being second":** Michael Collins, *Carrying
the Fire: An Astronaut's Journeys* (1974; 50th anniversary ed.,
Farrar, Straus and Giroux, 2019), Kindle.

111 **"that guy's seats are better":** Patrick O'Shaughnessy, host,
Invest Like the Best, podcast, episode 337, "Building Thrive

Capital," July 18, 2023, joincolossus.com/episodes/60539836
/kushner-building-thrive-capital?tab=transcript.

114 **Lawrence Yeo, once wrote:** Lawrence Yeo, "The Antidote
to Envy," *More to That* (blog), n.d., moretothat.com/the
-antidote-to-envy.

116 **go bankrupt in the future:** Sumit Agarwal, Vyacheslav
Mikhed, and Barry Scholnick, "Peers' Income and Financial
Distress: Evidence from Lottery Winners and Neighboring
Bankruptcies," *Review of Financial Studies* 33, no. 1 (January
2020): 433–72, academic.oup.com/rfs/article-abstract/33/1
/433/5488177.

116 **"Someone will always be getting richer":** Charlie Munger,
quoted in Morgan Housel, "FOMO the Worst Financial
Trait," Collaborative Fund, January 19, 2023, collabfund
.com/blog/fomo-the-worst-financial-trait.

117 **worse off by several metrics:** Jennifer Breheny Wallace,
*Never Enough: When Achievement Culture Becomes Toxic—
and What We Can Do About It* (Portfolio, 2023), Kindle.

Wealth Without Independence Is a Unique Form of Poverty

123 **twelve seasons in the NBA:** Celtics Wire, "How Antoine
Walker Lost $108,000,000, but Found His Way Again,"
Yahoo Sports, July 15, 2023, sports.yahoo.com/antoine
-walker-lost-108-000-090045760.html.

123 **"worry about money again in his life":** Bloomberg,
"Basketball Star Who Went Bankrupt Wishes He'd
Gotten an MBA," *InvestmentNews*, November 19, 2014,
investmentnews.com/industry-news/archive/basketball-star
-who-went-bankrupt-wishes-hed-gotten-an-mba-59681.

123 **a full-sized basketball court:** Lester Munson, "Antoine
Walker Wants Your 'Writ of Pity,'" ESPN.com, June 3, 2010,
espn.com/espn/commentary/news/story?page=munson
/100603.

124 **"I don't ever need to worry about money":** "Interview with
Former Pro Football Player and Math PhD Candidate John
Urschel," *MIT Faculty Newsletter* 30, no. 2 (November/
December 2017), web.mit.edu/fnl/volume/302/urschel
.html.

125 **"The more you have to lose"**: Nassim Taleb, *Skin in the Game: Hidden Asymmetries in Daily Life* (Random House, 2018).

125 **ousted from his company**: Benjamin Stupples, "Margin Calls, Lawsuits Squeeze Wealth of Leveraged Executives," *Bloomberg*, February 26, 2024, bloomberg.com/news /articles/2024-02-26/margin-calls-lawsuits-squeeze-wealth -of-leveraged-executives.

Social Debt

135 **"you gone outshine me?'"**: Frank Lucas, *Original Gangster* (Ebury, 2010), 243.

137 **one of the winners**: Elisabeth Ginsburg, "Lottery Winners Years Later," *New York Times*, January 31, 1993, nytimes .com/1993/01/31/nyregion/lottery-winners-years-later .html.

140 **Nerburn once wrote to his sons**: M. G. Bianco, *Letters to My Sons: A Humane Vision for Human Relationships* (CreateSpace, 2014).

Identity

149 **"Money is like gasoline"**: Tim O'Reilly, quoted in Cheng-Wei Hu, Weekly I/O#77, chengweihu.com/io/money-is-gasoline.

149 **before he became wealthy**: Harvey S. Firestone, *Men and Rubber: The Story of Business* (1926; repr., Latticework, 2023), 128.

150 **Graham has a saying**: Paul Graham, "Keep Your Identity Small," February 2009, *Paul Graham* (blog), paulgraham .com/identity.html.

152 **also linked to Alzheimer's disease**: Sonia Fernandez, "New Research Shows Genetic Mutation Known for Alzheimer's Disease Is Associated with Higher Fertility in Women," *The Current* (UC Santa Barbara), August 10, 2023, news .ucsb.edu/2023/021170/new-research-shows-genetic -mutation-known-alzheimers-disease-associated-higher.

154 **"a little smarter, a little quicker"**: CNBC, "Full Transcript from CNBC's 'Charlie Munger: A Life of Wit and Wisdom,'" CNBC.com, November 30, 2023, cnbc.com/amp/2023/11/30

/full-transcript-from-cnbcs-charlie-munger-a-life-of-wit-and
-wisdom-.html.

155 **"We are built with":** Dee Hock, quoted in Morgan Housel,
"Mental Liquidity," Collaborative Fund, March 29, 2023,
collabfund.com/blog/mental-liquidity.

Try Something New

159 **"I know what to ignore":** Safi Bahcall, *Loonshots: How to
Nurture the Crazy Ideas That Win Wars, Cure Diseases, and
Transform Industries* (St. Martin's, 2019).

159 **ignore everything else:** John M. Barry, *The Great Influenza:
The Epic Story of the Deadliest Plague in History* (Viking,
2004).

160 **half of Americans don't read books:** David Montgomery,
"54% of Americans Read a Book This Year," December 21,
2023, YouGov, today.yougov.com/entertainment/articles
/48239-54-percent-of-americans-read-a-book-this-year.

168 **"If you learn to enjoy":** Anthony De Mello, *The Way to Love*
(Doubleday, 1992).

Your Money and Your Kids

171 **"a rich father":** As told by Chris Davis.

171 **kids financially in the last year:** Faith Hill, "The New Age of
Endless Parenting," *Atlantic*, July 9, 2024, theatlantic.com
/family/archive/2024/07/modern-parenting-grown-children
/678942.

172 **"they have stocks and bonds":** Alice Schroeder, *The
Snowball: Warren Buffett and the Business of Life* (Bantam,
2008).

174 **blew the smoke into Billy's face:** Arthur T. Vanderbilt II,
Fortune's Children: The Fall of the House of Vanderbilt
(William Morrow, 1989), 26.

175 **"When a child cannot meet":** Jennifer Breheny Wallace,
Never Enough: When Achievement Culture Becomes Toxic
(Portfolio, 2023).

176 **"I've come to believe that upward":** Rob Henderson,
Troubled: A Memoir of Foster Care, Family, and Social Class
(Gallery Books, 2024).

178 **for Democrats, it's nine in ten:** Alan Cooperman, "Most U.S.
Parents Pass Along Their Religion and Politics to Their
Children," Pew Research Center, May 10, 2023, pewresearch
.org/short-reads/2023/05/10/most-us-parents-pass-along
-their-religion-and-politics-to-their-children.

Spreadsheets Don't Care About Your Feelings

182 **his mom selling her longtime home:** Jason Zweig, "The Real
Value of a Home," *Jason Zweig* (blog), November 30, 2015,
jasonzweig.com/the-real-value-of-a-home.

183 **"your foot to is good music":** *Jazz*, directed by Ken Burns
(PBS, 2001).

The Finer Things

185 **Author Rory Sutherland writes:** Rory Sutherland, *Alchemy:
The Dark Art and Curious Science of Creating Magic in
Brands, Business, and Life* (Mariner Books, 2019).

185 **Department of Agriculture that read:** Jamie Catherwood
(@InvestorAmnesia), "Calvin Coolidge took the meaning of
'frugal' to another level . . . The juxtaposition of Coolidge's
cost-cutting measures with today's federal spending is
pretty insane. Taken from the @FinanceMuseum
Summer issue." X, November 21, 2023, twitter.com
/InvestorAmnesia/status/1727001307100406152.

186 **a crazier example:** Ron Chernow, *Titan: The Life of John
D. Rockefeller, Sr.* (Vintage, 2004).

189 **"blow $500,000 that way":** Alice Schroeder, *The
Snowball: Warren Buffett and the Business of Life* (Bantam,
2008).

189 **for a $1 hot dog:** *Barron's*, "The $1000 Hot Dog," posted by
Davis Funds, n.d., davisfunds.com/insights/video/hotdog
-video-barron.

The Life Cycle of Greed and Fear

193 **James Weldon Johnson on New York City:** *New York:
A Documentary Film*, directed by Ric Burns (PBS,
1999–2003).

How to Be Miserable Spending Your Money

205 **"Don't do cocaine":** Charlie Munger, quoted in Morgan Housel, "Charlie Munger's Humorous Advice," The Motley Fool, April 5, 2017, fool.com/investing/general/2008/02/22 /charlie-mungers-humorous-advice.aspx.

The Luckier You Are, the Nicer You Should Be

211 **that stopped me in my tracks:** Tae Kim (@firstadopter), "This is a good story," Threads, July 15, 2023, threads.net /@firstadopter/post/CuuWTSSuusD?igshid=MTc4MmM1 YmI2Ng%3D%3D.

215 **Benjamin Franklin didn't say honesty:** Thanks to Charlie Munger for this one.

01 14